AF669066

EDUCATION: Planning and Human Development

EDUCATION

Planning and Human Development

(In 8 Volumes)

Higher Education in a Globalising World

(Volume 3)

V.C. PANDEY

ISHA BOOKS
DELHI—110 033

EDUCATION: Planning and Human Development
(Education)

Rs. 7000 (Set in 8 Vols.)

ISBN: 81-8205-006-5 (Set)
ISBN: 81-8205-009-X (Vol. 3)

Published in 2003 in India by
Isha Books, D-43, Prithviraj Road
Adarsh Nagar, Delhi-110 033

Lasertypesetting by: Varsha Graphics, Delhi
Printed at: Chawla Offset Press, Delhi

Preface

Higher education has always operated within a global and multi-cultural arena. But the environment has changed dramatically over the past decade. We now live in the era of instant global communications. Many higher education institutions see themselves as international bodies. Reports from organisations such as United Nations Educational, Scientific & Cultural Organisation (UNESCO), the World Bank and the Organisation for Economic Co-operation and Development (OECD) acknowledge the crucial role for education in economic development throughout the world. In these reports the roles for higher education in economic development, the globalisation of the world economy, the development of a knowledge-based society and the education and training of a skilled and flexible workforce are seen as crucial.

Academic and academic related staff in higher education are increasingly likely to become involved in a variety of ways in educational activities with an international dimension whether as policy makers, advisors, members of research or teaching groups or as individual practitioners. This increasing international participation has had the effect of both emphasising existing problems of ethical issues arising out of academic work and of raising new ones; there is growing concern expressed as more examples of unethical behaviour are made public.

It is indisputable that the world as a whole must develop on a sustainable basis and in a way which seeks to ensure its free and fair enjoyment by all, both present and future generations. Not withstanding the need to respect cultural diversity, increased interaction creates the need to seek global acceptance of fundamental rights, in particular, through educational opportunities. Furthermore, higher education cannot shirk its responsibilities to human progress and the immediate need to attack world problems of poverty, illiteracy and disease. These principles must underpin the universities' mission statements and inform the practice of all organisations both within and outside higher education.

This book has considered the role of higher education in an increasingly inter-connected world, a role which is becoming more and more recognised and integrated into the process of economic development. It has also sought to look at development in broader terms than just economic and in a way that reflects higher education's traditional roles and values. While this process may generate apparent tensions, the book seeks to advise on means of managing such tensions.

Editor

Contents

1

Introduction

The impressive development of education in the latter half of the twentieth century, sometimes termed the 'education explosion', and the very significant rise in the average level of education of the world population constitute one of the major changes of global scope. Its impact in the economic, social, cultural and political fields is still far from being fully apparent. Eventually it will prove to be much greater than we imagine.

It is the development of higher education - whose rate of expansion has been the most spectacular - that has been one of the decisive factors in the progress of education as a whole and the remarkable advance of knowledge. It is this development that, in the space of a few decades, has brought about an unprecedented increase in capacities for the advance and spread of knowledge and its practical applications and for technological innovation. This great quantitative change over such a short period has not been accompanied by conceptual and qualitative changes of comparable scale and depth, appropriate to the new situations, requirements and needs.

On the threshold of a new century, higher education must come to terms in its teaching, research and scholarship with the effects and consequences of the globalization (of communications and, as yet only partially, of trade) and internationalization of the life of societies, the development of information technologies, the rapidly evolving structure of employment needs and the steady increase in the demand for highly qualified personnel.

At the same time, the need for refresher courses and further education to broaden general knowledge and occupational skills, and for career-change retraining, is becoming increasingly urgent, so that higher education has to be more responsive to this task and make it an integral part of its activities. 'Coming to terms with' means not just adjusting, but, above all, anticipating, influencing, guiding.

Higher education must strengthen and target more effectively its contribution to sustainable and mutually supportive human development - in particular through sustained efforts to promote the sharing of knowledge, to the reduction of inequalities at the international and the national levels, to combating exclusion and unemployment, and to the eradication of poverty and the various forms of exploitation and discrimination.

The growing importance of knowledge in the world today and the ever greater numbers of people being trained at the higher level has increased higher education's responsibility to and its influence within society. In order fully to assume this responsibility and this role, higher education needs to change, as is clearly shown by the conclusions of the regional conferences on higher education held between 1996 and 1998 in Havana,

Dakar, Tokyo, Palermo and Beirut and all the studies made in preparation for the World Conference. To that end, it needs the assistance and increased support of the whole of society, and of the State in particular. Not the least of the contradictions and paradoxes that are a feature of the present era are those concerning higher education.

Never has the expansion of education in general and higher education in particular been so necessary to society for its normal functioning, its development and its economic, social, cultural, moral and political well-being as it is at present. Yet society seems reluctant to give education, especially higher education, the resources that would enable it to fulfil its mission satisfactorily in the service of that society. If this contradiction is not overcome, its negative consequences will, in the twenty-first century, seriously affect the different sectors and diverse aspects of social life.

This situation is not unrelated to a tendency to approach questions of education and higher education as if educational institutions were economic entities producing marketable goods and services. It is with reference to this approach that George Papadopoulos speaks of 'the turmoil which has been created as a result of the application to education of the tenets of a free market philosophy based on choice and competition'. It is important to dispel the ambiguities and confusion reigning here. The laws of the market and the logic of competition cannot be applied to education, including higher education.

There is every justification for expecting education to use the resources made available to it as rationally as possible in the light of its purpose and tasks, and for higher education more particularly to be accountable to society. The financing of education, or of higher education, cannot however be subject to the criteria of the market and competition, whether between educational institutions or between such institutions and economic or other entities. Education is not a branch of the economy, and neither the educational process, nor its ultimate purposes, nor its results or 'production', are comparable with those of the economy.

It is in itself a vital function, an essential sector of society and a condition of society's existence. Without it there is no society. It has at one and the same time cultural, social, economic, civic and ethical functions. It concerns the whole of society and its various sectors, which all need it. It ensures the continuity of society, and passes on the knowledge and skills, the norms developed and the experience accumulated by humanity over the course of its history. It trains the capacities which enable society to move ahead, to progress, to innovate and to change, including in the economic sphere.

Unless it is to risk jeopardizing its normal functioning and progress, society cannot reduce its support for education by cut-backs. It should be doing the opposite, in view of the increasing importance to society of education in general and higher education in particular and the steady increase of the number of participants in the educational process. The current worldwide trend towards a reduction in the role of the State in the economic field cannot be automatically extended to the field of education and cannot justify direct or indirect pressure for cuts in public expenditure on higher education and the transfer of a large part of the financial burden to families, which would only accentuate inequality of access to higher education.

In the 1960s, some economists sought to demonstrate the high rates of return to society of the advanced levels of education systems, regarded as contributing directly to the training of the labour force and highly skilled human resources, and thereby to economic growth. They accordingly encouraged investment in these levels. For some time now, other economists have attempted to show that higher education yields low returns as compared with basic education, drawing conclusions for the distribution of public expenditure among the different levels of the education system.

There is indeed a need to reflect on the consequences for a modern economy - with its high technicity and sophisticated technology, its need for innovation, in turn requiring continual progress in research and highly qualified personnel in the various fields, especially new fields, who need not only to keep their knowledge up to date but to progress, improve and innovate personally - if higher education with its 'low rates of return' were to have its resources cut back and were thus obliged to reduce staff costs, and hence enrolments and research work, and to abandon any idea of renewing facilities, laboratory equipment, etc.

We might then conclude that strictly economic criteria are a too narrow and inadequate basis on which to form a correct opinion as to the importance of higher education to society and even to the economy. Account should also be taken of the fact that the great majority of the men and women whose activity will be a determining factor in shaping the twenty-first century are at present in higher education institutions, or will be educated there over the next few decades, and that the research conducted by those institutions will be at the root of many of the innovations that will carry the economy forward.

The problems of higher education and education in general are one of the great challenges confronting society in the approaches to the twenty-first century. Higher education, for its part, is faced with the challenge of preparing itself to fulfil its mission adequately in a world in transformation and to meet the needs and requirements of twenty-first century society, which will be a society of knowledge, information and education. For several years now, a great debate on the problems of higher education, organized and led by UNESCO, has been under way in various parts of the world. Numerous consultations and meetings have taken place, with the participation of academics, higher education decision-makers, students and representatives of their organizations and of various social actors.

Missions of higher education

The paramount mission of higher education is to serve the human person and society. Through its work of research and enquiry, its courses of study and training, its co-operative activities and its partnerships with various social actors, higher education is called upon to make a key contribution to opening up and highlighting new paths to a better future for society and the individual, and to give direction and shape to that future. The development of capacities to 'explore the future' and anticipate thus deserves the full attention of higher education. From this standpoint, it has a twofold mission:

(a) participating actively in the solving of major global, regional and local problems, such as poverty, hunger, illiteracy, social exclusion, the exacerbation of inequalities at international and national levels, the widening of the gap between industrialized and developing countries, and protection of the environment, and

(b) working tirelessly, in particular by drawing up alternative proposals and recommendations, to promote: sustainable human development; the sharing of knowledge; universal respect for human rights; equal rights for women and men; justice and the application of democratic principles within its own institutions and in society; understanding among nations, and among ethnic, religious, cultural and other groups; a culture of peace and non-violence; and 'intellectual and moral solidarity'.

The traditional mission of maintaining, increasing and diffusing knowledge through research and intellectual creation, and teaching and spreading knowledge in various ways, is fundamental. It concerns science and technology and the social and human sciences and implies taking account of the needs of society and its economic, social and cultural development as well as of major world trends foreseeable for the years ahead. It includes the task of developing endogenous capacities for acquiring and applying existing knowledge and creating new knowledge.

In regard to teaching proper, its task is to educate responsible, enlightened and active citizens and highly qualified specialists, while ensuring all-round education and well-rounded individual development, including sound training in both specialist and basic disciplines together with a good general education, and the task of helping students to learn to learn and to learn to be enterprising. This mission has an important ethical and civic aspect, for it means helping students to acquire knowledge, skills, attitudes, values and abilities that will incline them to act as responsible, committed citizens, It has yet another aspect which will in future become increasingly important - namely, the updating and improvement of knowledge and skills, and the further education or career-change retraining of graduates or non-graduates.

One of the most important missions of higher education in society is its cultural and ethical mission. Higher education is required to preserve and assert cultural identity, promote the propagation and creation of cultural values, protect and encourage cultural diversity and participate actively in the development of intercultural understanding and harmony and the mutual enrichment of cultures. The transmission of cultural values, which is bound up with ethical considerations, should permeate all courses in higher education.

One of the major missions of higher education is to contribute to the implementation of lifelong learning for all, to become an essential element and driving force in such education and, to that end, to change and transform itself. With this in view, and more generally, higher education has a great responsibility in regard to the whole of the education system and educational activities in society.

By strengthening its links with the different levels and forms of education, by stepping up its educational research, by strengthening and extending its training courses for education personnel and participating in the preparation, follow-up and evaluation of education policies and reforms, it has a role to play in helping attain the goal of education for all and in improving the quality and increasing the effectiveness of the educational process in its various aspects.

Constructive Interaction with Society

Constructive interaction of the principal social actors with higher education, with due respect for its purpose and its institutional autonomy, is becoming increasingly necessary to enable it to fulfil its missions to optimum effect. This presupposes that higher education is aware of the needs and aspirations of society and the various groups and of longer-term world trends.

The interaction of higher education with the State, parliament and the government seems particularly important, as also with the world of work and the media, which thus have a share of responsibility for the situation of higher education, its development, renewal and improvement.

Interaction presupposes that each party involved takes initiatives or action of interest to the other party or parties. Generally speaking, the effort required of higher education institutions to develop and optimize interaction with society as a whole is implicit in the missions of higher education, as these emerge from the texts adopted by the regional conferences.

As regards relations between higher education and the world of work, a keenly debated question worldwide, higher education has a responsibility to 'anticipate the signals of the world of work' and 'evaluate the possibilities of co-operation with the productive sector', it being necessary to 'improve links with the world of work'.

Interactive partnerships with the productive sector must be encouraged by means of 'reactive and proactive approaches'. This presupposes adjustments in higher education courses 'to meet the needs of the workplace and ensure that new disciplines and specializations are incorporated into its content', and that higher education institutions play an active part in helping to shape the labour market by identifying, independently of the immediate economic interests of business, new local and regional needs and in setting up retraining and career-switching courses.

Higher education therefore has an active role to play and is called upon to act by anticipating the needs of society and the individual, by determining its long-term directions on the basis of social demand and not the labour market and manpower planning. It should help students acquire, in addition to professional qualifications, a general education and transferable skills and competences so as to increase their employability in a knowledge society and broaden their knowledge of economic and social development. Interaction, and not just the systematic adaptation of higher education, partnership, and hence a relationship of equal partners and not subordination to the market, must characterize relations between higher education and the world of work. The state has an important role to play in encouraging such interaction.

For higher education, relations with the State and a constructive partnership with it are of the utmost importance. It is up to the State, in consultation with higher education, to implement policies and legislation establishing optimum conditions for the functioning and development of higher education, to respect and promote the autonomy of its institutions and academic freedoms, to help establish procedures making it easier for these institutions to be accountable to society for their activities and the use of the resources made available to them, and to temper the excesses of economistic approaches.

Partnership is a key means of developing constructive interaction with the principal social actors, which should mobilize 'to bring about a fundamental change in higher education on the basis of the establishment of a new "social consensus" in order to help higher education institutions meet the needs of sustainable human development'.Constructive partnerships between these institutions and the government and the economic sector are crucial if higher education is to change. 'Real partnerships must therefore be set up with public and private institutions'. Active support to ensure that higher education has adequate resources, particularly financial, is a basic aspect in the relationship and interaction between it and the main social actors.

Higher education's growing needs lead its institutions to seek additional sources of funding. Their efforts deserve the encouragement and support of society and, above all, of the authorities. Nevertheless, as higher education is 'a common good', 'a public asset'. and has to play 'a key role in opening new futures', 'the State cannot but assume responsibility for its financing'; 'it should take the main responsibility for financing higher education'; the government is supposed to ensure 'stable funding schemes'; and 'the State should remain the main party responsible for funding higher education'. This principle of state responsibility for the financing of higher education now has as its corollaries

(i) the accountability of higher education institutions to society for their activities and for the use made of the resources it places at their disposal, and

(ii) sustained imaginative efforts on the part of these institutions to obtain additional sources of financing and to undertake their own income-generating activities.

Diversification and Flexibility

The acceleration in the advance of knowledge means that individuals must constantly update their knowledge. What is more, the advance of knowledge leads increasingly to technological innovations which disrupt the employment structure, create personnel needs in new fields and specializations, increase the needs in certain existing fields while in many cases altering the qualifications and skills required, and at the same time reduce or do away with personnel needs in certain fields and in certain traditional occupations. This twofold process, which will become more and more marked, makes it necessary for higher education constantly to update its courses and the range of subjects taught and to review the educational process so that it contributes to learning to learn and learning to be enterprising.

Furthermore, it places higher education before the task of implementing both new courses of the traditional type and an increasingly wide variety of courses of new types for graduates or non-graduates who are seeking to update or refresh their knowledge and skills, to retrain, to change career or to broaden their general education.

In many countries higher education has already applied itself to this task to varying extents, and some of its institutions have taken the initiative of establishing partnerships with companies and other social actors and organizing training courses for specific socio-economic or purely cultural purposes. However, it is now a question of regarding this activity as an organic function whose importance is bound to increase.

Flexibility and the capacity to cope quickly enough with the evolution of needs, and to make the necessary internal changes, to anticipate this trend and help shape its direction, are becoming characteristics necessary to higher education if it is to accomplish its mission in society to the full.

Another socio-economic trend is a powerful factor in the expansion of higher education. On the one hand, an ever-increasing number and proportion of jobs and activities require knowledge and skills of a high level. Higher studies thus become necessary to fill these jobs, and the social demand for higher education is tending to increase continually as the role of advanced rational knowledge in human activity increases. On the other hand, in increasingly complex societies, participation in the political, social and cultural life of the city, the exercise of human rights, and everyday life which is also increasingly complex, incline and encourage young people and adults of all ages to broaden their general education throughout their lives and to acquire the knowledge and skills required in a knowledge society.

These processes have two major consequences, which are already operative and which will lead in the long run to a radical change in all educational activity in both quantitative and qualitative terms.

First, together with the substantial expansion of secondary education, which has already become almost universal in the developed countries and is on the way to becoming so in a growing number of other countries, these processes are at the origin of growth rates in higher education even more spectacular than those in secondary education. Their combined effect, reinforced by the new opportunities opened up by the information and communication technologies for the widening of access to higher education, is resulting in a strong trend towards the generalization of higher education, either sooner or later according to the country. This generalization will not resemble that of secondary education and will not lead to direct promotion for all from secondary to higher education without a break. It means that practically everyone will go through one form or another of higher/post-secondary education, but at various stages in their lives. It will often happen in new and increasingly diverse ways, with increasingly varied, and even customized, study objectives, entry paths and chosen course lengths. The only solution will be to see higher education institutions as a place for lifelong education. In view of the nature of the factors which are at the origin of this tendency towards the generalization of higher education, which will benefit people at one period of their lives or another, the trend seems irreversible in the long run and stands out as one of the major challenges higher education and societies will have to meet in the twenty-first century. It is important that they consider this prospect and prepare for it with imagination and realism.

Secondly, in the light of the above-mentioned processes and trends, it is becoming necessary to rethink education as a whole, since none of its levels or forms, including higher education, can be regarded as truly final any longer, and since its structures and courses cannot remain fixed once and for all, but will have to evolve, vary and become more flexible in order to respond to the evolution of societies, needs and aspirations or, better still, to anticipate and help shape their direction.

For higher education, from the institutional, functional and curricular standpoints, this radical change means its full integration in an overall project for continuing or lifelong education. 'The nature of present-day knowledge, owing to its constant renewal and breathtaking expansion, is in keeping with the concept of lifelong education; the lifelong education model must be integrated without delay.

Diversification and flexibility in higher education - aspects that are closely interlinked - are a major feature of lifelong education. They relate, in particular, to objectives, access, course content, institutional structures, fields covered, course types and length, delivery systems, methods and techniques used and staff employed on teaching duties. Flexibility also means the capacity of institutions to meet new needs quickly, or even to anticipate them, to make structures flexible and fluid, to adjust entrance criteria to take account of experience in working life.

Distance education, education at the workplace, and especially the new information and communication technologies, considerably extend higher education's opportunities to apply the concept of lifelong education. It is important that the authorities and the economic sector help it to equip itself with these technologies and that its institutions train their personnel to make full use of them for teaching, learning and research. For this, it is essential to step up international co-operation, on behalf of the developing countries in particular.

The prospect of a durable expansion of higher education and its integration into a comprehensive project of lifelong education for all, with all that this implies, makes it necessary for higher education institutions, governments and other social actors to mobilize and work together to devise measures to strengthen the admission capacities of higher education. It is important that these capacities correspond to the evolution, anticipated as far as possible, of successive entrance flows and match the diversity of students and their needs.

Preparing the necessary measures entails providing the means, and in particular the funds. In this connection, while States are reminded - as they have been by the regional conferences - that it is their duty to provide higher education with the resources it needs, and while institutions are encouraged to seek additional sources of financing, it is recommended that a National Fund for higher education be set up in the countries which consider it appropriate. Such a Fund, which would be administered in accordance with the legislation obtaining in each State, would be maintained by contributions from all sectors, organizations and firms needing graduates and the services of higher education.

The changes to be made in higher education so that it can be fully integrated in a comprehensive project of lifelong education entail changes in other levels and forms of education: above all, secondary education.

The trend towards generalization of the latter and the gradual opening of the traditional branches and courses to adults who have graduated from secondary schools or have the experience and knowledge required, together with the development in higher education of courses for adults - graduates or non-graduates, create a new situation. This situation is rapidly opening the way to a generalized possibility of entering higher education at various stages in life and not necessarily just after secondary education. This makes it possible and necessary to provide young people with an education that will enable them, on leaving secondary school, to choose freely between pursuing their studies without interruption or entering working life. This implies a twofold purpose for secondary education - preparing students to enter working life and at the same time preparing them to enter higher education. This twofold purpose in turn implies considerable changes in the overall direction and content of secondary education, starting with general secondary education.

Except in very few countries, most of the students at this level enter general secondary schools, which in most cases just prepare them for the pursuit of higher studies. In this connection, the trend observed here and there towards, on the one hand, including in general secondary education elements of applied science and some practical knowledge and skills and, on the other, strengthening general education and developing more transferable skills in technical and vocational courses - in other words, the tendency of general education and technical and vocational education to draw closer together - deserves to be actively supported.

Admission to higher education of graduates from technical and vocational education, when this occurs, helps to consolidate this trend. With this prospect in view, it becomes necessary to think in terms of a new approach to pre-university education for the twenty-first century, which would provide a redefined general education incorporating and bringing together literary, scientific and technological culture and offering a broad introduction to the main fields of human activity together with a good grounding in one of those fields.

Secondary schooling would thus prepare students to enter higher education, while qualifying them to enter working life in their chosen field, including a wide choice of occupations, it being understood that those who chose to enter working life would retain the guaranteed right to resume their studies and take up traditional or other courses in higher education, their work experience being counted as an asset. This will clarify the educational and social role of secondary education and its specific identity; it will help to go beyond the dichotomy of general and vocational secondary education, integrating them better into the comprehensive project for lifelong education by attaching educational value to working experience and facilitating the interlinking of the world of education, including higher education, and the world of work.

By changing itself, higher education will trigger a change in the education system, more especially in secondary education. It will make for greater coherence and better 'vertical' and 'horizontal' continuity between the various levels and forms of education and will thus promote the contribution of the education system as a whole to the implementation of lifelong education.

Access to Higher Education

The conditions governing such access reflect in large measure national policies in regard to higher education and, in some respects, to education generally. The

Universal Declaration of Human Rights proclaims in Article 26 (1) 'Everyone has the right to education [...] higher education shall be equally accessible to all on the basis of merit'. In the UNESCO Convention against Discrimination in Education, Article 4.a, the states parties undertake to 'make higher education equally accessible to all on the basis of individual capacity'. And the International Covenant on Economic, Social and Cultural Rights stipulates in Article 13, paragraph 2(c), that 'higher education shall be made equally accessible to all, on the basis of capacity, by every appropriate means, and in particular by the progressive introduction of free education'.

The terms 'merit' and 'individual capacity' can be taken to mean - among other things - adequate preparation, demonstrated work drive and ability, and a clear and well-motivated choice in favour of higher studies in this or that field, practical experience constituting an asset. The term 'equally accessible' to all reflects the goal of equity, which is the first principle that should govern access to higher education.

The International Covenant elaborates on this principle, adding 'by every appropriate means, and in particular by the progressive introduction of free education', in the first place for those who have the 'capacity' but not the 'means'. Those who have both the capacity and the means can pay all or a part of the cost. Those who have only the means must endeavour to acquire the merit and the capacity.

In a democratic system - the only system in which higher education can be radically changed, this applies to both public and private institutions. And in both cases it is a matter not just for the authorities, but for society as a whole. Social stability is based on justice. And on the observance of human rights.

Nowadays, despite the significant broadening of access, inequalities still exist. Their origins are various - geographical, economic and social. They also include the persistent influence of elitism. These inequalities particularly affect women, rural populations and the various disadvantaged groups. They concern access to education, to the teaching profession and to posts of responsibility.

Reasons of equity, but also social and economic considerations and the goal of lifelong education for all, make it vital that there should be sustained and resolute efforts to widen and democratize access to, and increase rates of participation in, higher education. Everyone should be able, at any stage in life, to resume and pursue studies and have 'an opportunity of returning to university life'. It is important to extend and diversify opportunities for every citizen to benefit from higher education, skills and knowledge.

Diversification of the demand implies institutional diversification, new policies and flexibility in regard to access. Special measures are required to facilitate access for those who have entered working life or dropped out prematurely. Goal-oriented policies are essential to increase the number and rate of participation of women in higher studies, in teaching and other responsible posts in higher education, as also in careers in science and technology. Special measures on behalf of various underprivileged groups are also necessary.

Open learning, distance education and the new information and communication technologies offer further opportunities of widening access to higher education, especially for new social categories. It is important to make full use of this potential for educational purposes. It devolves on the State and the higher education institutions to devise and implement specific policies to this end.

The widening and democratization of access to higher education must today be conceived in the context of lifelong education for all, in the realization of which higher education has a crucial role to play. The diversification of institutions, of traditional-type courses, and above all of courses for updating or upgrading general and professional knowledge and skills and for retraining and career reorientation for graduates or non-graduates, make for wider and more flexible access and contribute to lifelong learning.

This development creates conditions facilitating renewed access at various stages in life, and not necessarily just after completion of secondary studies. It thus changes the composition of the higher education population from the standpoint of age and socio-occupational category, the student body being likely to include an increasing proportion of adults with experience of working life and greater maturity.

A concern for equity requires the implementation of specific policies providing for economic, social and educational measures upstream - as it were - of the educational process, so as to improve the chances of success of many children from disadvantaged environments and modest backgrounds and enable them to acquire the necessary preparation for proceeding to higher education, thereby ensuring that society benefits from all the potential resources of intelligence and talent of the population.

Protagonists in Higher Education

Students and teachers are the main protagonists in higher education, particularly in the teaching/learning process. Their interaction is central to the activities of higher education institutions. The development of the new information technologies opens up possibilities barely imaginable not so long ago for teaching and learning and for the diversification of higher education, and it is significantly changing the roles of teacher and student in the educational process as well as the characteristics of that process.

Nevertheless, it does not lessen the importance of direct human contacts, between student and teacher and among students themselves. The student/teacher contact creates a relationship which becomes an active and often determining factor in the quality and the results of the teaching/learning process.

Any society that thinks about its future should attach the utmost importance to everything concerning students - their education and training, their state of mind, their aspirations and needs, the values that inspire them, their living and working conditions. In a rapidly and radically changing world, it is essential for students to acquire, in the course of their studies, qualities such as the capacity to analyse complex situations, creativity, initiative, an entrepreneurial spirit and a sense of responsibility, along with a good general education, a sound training in the basic disciplines of their chosen field and skills as transferable as possible in order to enhance their employability, as well as the qualities of active citizens with a sense of human solidarity so as to enable them to become autonomous and direct their own lives and make a useful contribution towards a better future for society.

It is therefore important that students be encouraged to play an active role in higher education institutions, that this role be recognized, as also that of their organizations, that they be allowed to participate in the framing of policies and decision-making concerning higher education and the designing of courses, and thus have a hand in shaping their own education. Such participation is necessary for their well-rounded development. At the same time, they should have the benefit of guidance and counselling services, remedial classes, an introduction to research, and measures enabling them to improve their living conditions.

Everything that concerns students interests teachers and vice versa. The academic qualifications of teachers, their ability to teach, their working and living conditions, their human and moral qualities and their general educational background have a crucial influence on the results of the teaching/learning process and the general and specialized education of students.

The teacher is the cornerstone of any higher education system. The spectacular expansion of higher education, its evolution in the direction of lifelong education and the diversification of its institutions and courses, of its delivery systems, of the needs it will have to meet, of the ages and experience of its students, change the traditional role of the teacher and diversify the teacher's tasks accordingly, calling for the development of new approaches to teaching.

With the faster progress of knowledge and techniques, this makes teaching more complex, but also more stimulating. Among other things, the ability to use the new information technologies for teaching and research is becoming increasingly necessary in the teaching profession.

The question of the education and further education of teachers in higher education, including their professional education, is taking on new aspects and increased importance, and specific measures, including the setting up of special facilities and networks, seem necessary for this purpose.

The participation of teachers in research and the linking of teaching and research are also becoming essential to ensure the quality and effectiveness of higher education, to contribute to the progress of knowledge and to develop endogenous capacities for research and R&D. The participation of the teachers in the working out of policies and course contents for higher education, as in decision-making concerning it, is essential if it is to run smoothly, but also if it is to change. Participation must be increased and the teachers' needs must be taken into account.

The improvement of teachers' living and working conditions is a task that concerns many countries and deserves the full attention of the governments and the whole of society. The implementation of policies concerning higher education teaching staff, their initial and further education, their recruitment, careers, working and living conditions, is an essential aspect of any higher education policy.

The academic mobility of teachers and students at the national, regional and international levels is an important factor in their education and personal development, in the sharing of knowledge, in the mutual appreciation of cultures and intellectual and moral solidarity, in bringing peoples closer together and, at regional level, in regional integration. The encouragement of academic mobility by governments and higher education institutions should be a part of national educational, scientific and cultural policies. Application of the regional conventions and of the International Recommendation on the Recognition of Studies, Diplomas and Degrees and the development of networks of institutions are regarded as important in this connection.

Autonomy and Accountability

Autonomy presupposes accountability to society. Institutional autonomy and academic freedoms are necessary for the effective functioning of the higher education system, for the strengthening of its capacity to change and anticipate, for the carrying out of its watch-tower or observatory functions, for the assertion of its moral authority in the debate on the great ethical problems and the major issues of global significance, but also for its development as a place where democracy can be practised and promoted. It must be added that the academic freedoms which, in a way, serve as a justification and basis for the critical function of higher education presuppose the observance of certain principles and norms, while laying upon higher education institutions the duty of objectivity, impartiality and intellectual rigour.

Research Development

Research is a fundamental mission and a major function of higher education. Higher education institutions contain a large proportion of the personnel educated for intellectual creation - in many countries the majority of such personnel. It is therefore essential that this potential be turned fully to account, not only for teaching purposes, but also in order to contribute through research in science and technology and in the social and human sciences to the advance of knowledge, to the creation of new knowledge, to cultural development and fulfilment, to the solving of the problems with which society is faced, to sustainable human development and to the spreading of the ideas of peace, democracy and protection of the environment. This is the duty, the responsibility and the function of higher education and its personnel, the teaching personnel in particular.

Ethical considerations should be taken into account in research work. Research and intellectual creation are necessary to ensure education of a high standard that is up to date and to develop a critical, innovative approach, creativity, the desire to advance, not to be content with what one already knows. Co-operation in a wide diversity of forms among higher education institutions at the national, regional and international levels - in particular through the creation and development of networks, and appropriate interaction with other social actors, public and private - are means of supporting and furthering research.

UNESCO and the regional organizations, as well as the international and regional specialized non-governmental organizations, have a special responsibility in the promotion of such co-operation.Higher education institutions must have sufficient resources for research. The State has a major responsibility in the funding of research, but other social actors also have a duty to aid these institutions. For their part, the institutions must be prepared to account for the use made of the resources, and to seek for themselves new sources of financing. Anticipation is an important task of higher education. What is involved is anticipating the needs and requirements of the future and not merely adapting to those of the present. In order to perform this task, higher education must strengthen its own capacity for anticipation. Thinking ahead and forecasting must inspire its courses and research work, and likewise its management. Anticipation will enable higher education to play an active role in society, particularly in regard to the new social and environmental needs, as well as in the field of education generally, and to help society shape the future and master its own destiny.

Contribution of Higher Education

A major role for higher education today relates to its contribution to education as a whole. In a fundamental sense, the requirement to adjust is true of all areas of education, as the various sectors, institutions and systems try to cope with unprecedented challenges. We will not understand the needs of higher education in a vacuum, but as part of an interconnected system where the changes in one part intimately affect all the other parts. This is particularly true of higher education whose institutions depend on the other sectors for their students and staff, but which, in their turn, develop the new knowledge and understandings, and also the new paradigms, by which we seek to explain and predict, as well as preparing for many of the professions.

It is only in the nature of the changes affecting education as a whole that we can consider the impact on particular sectors and, especially, the interaction between sectors that is our concern here. It is worth taking a little time to consider the impact of change on education and the ways in which the area as a whole seeks to respond. To assess realistically the contribution of higher education to the development of education systems as a whole demands a careful look at the needs of those systems.

A clear sign of the changed significance of education is in the priority it now is given-nationally and internationally Countries place a high priority on education as a major means of being or becoming competitive in a tough global economic environment. This is often stated in terms of the necessity of developing a productive work-force. Similarly, international organizations see education as the key to further human and social development. For organizations such as UNESCO, this is scarcely surprising as education has been a key part of its charter for the fifty-plus years of its existence. It is illuminating that bodies with a hard-headed economic charter, such as OECD and the World Bank, now proclaim the same message.

OECD has now been substantially involved in education for three decades and it is easy to forget that it began with a charter directed only at economic reconstruction in a war-damaged Europe, its only link to education being programmes for training technicians for industry. It was the economic needs which persuaded the organization that a broad education base was a necessity for significant economic advance.

The World Bank began with a similarly focussed economic agenda. It did not make any investment in education until its first loan for that purpose in 1963, but its experience has caused it to expand that commitment.

The Bank is now the largest source of external financing for education in developing countries, even though it sees its main contribution as advice to help governments in developing their education policies. The Bank's finance thus plays an important double role: directly supporting educational development; and also providing leverage on government policies, to the same end.

Higher living standards, better health, increased productivity, improved well-being for women and their families, and good government all depend on widespread education. In an era of rapid technological change and international economic integration, an educated, adaptable work-force enables countries to prosper. The reverse is also true: countries without such a work-force are liable to be left behind and shut out of this prosperity.

The commonality of views between international bodies is significant and will have a powerful influence on governments and the future directions of educational policy and practice at all levels. This commonality was both demonstrated and extended in 1990 by the World Conference on Education for All, held at Jomtien, Thailand, under the joint auspices of UNESCO, UNICEF, UNDP and the World Bank. Jomtien emphasized the severity of the need: after almost fifty years of international and national effort, progress was uneven and in many cases non-existent.

The 1970 figure for illiterates in the 15+ age group was 760 million; by 1990 it had grown to 882 million and it was estimated that it would reach 912 million by 2000. Other key indicators were equally disturbing. What was equally a matter of concern was the so-called 'convergence of disadvantage', the concept that illiteracy was intimately linked to other social indicators, such as infant mortality, reduced life expectancy, and poor housing and employment opportunities.

After four decades of successes and failures it has become abundantly clear that economic, socio-cultural and environmental processes are closely linked; development or decay along one dimension profoundly affects the others. The pivotal determinant of the success of these programs and policies will be whether a country's population possesses the appropriate basic skills and knowledge.

UNESCO established the International Consultative Forum on Education for All, (ICFEA), to promote and monitor progress towards Education for All goals during the 1990s. From the Jomtien Conference came the broad-based international commitment to a massive programme of 'Basic Education for All', to which the major international bodies, plus national governments, are deeply committed. While this programme is explicitly aimed at the developing countries, where the need is clear and urgent, a similar emphasis applies more generally. Further, while the explicit focus is on basic education, this requires particular attention from higher education, partly in its role of professional education and training, but even more importantly through its intellectual contribution.

The Jomtien Conference raised a vision of a world divided between the nations who had successfully developed their education systems and those who had not and could not. This divide is deep and, on the evidence, could grow deeper, raising strong concerns on the health and sustainability of the world society. The divide between the 'haves' and 'have-nots' is actually more pervasive and fundamental than between rich and poor countries. It consists of the gap within as well as between countries which is becoming more evident between those who have developed the capacities to prosper in what Drucker has called the 'knowledge society' and those who, for whatever reason, have not done so.

In our current education, success in schooling is heavily dependent on social background, with the socially deprived performing more poorly at all stages and with the disparity increasing with time. With the need to extend old areas of the curriculum, to reach new areas and to reach higher standards in both, the task of making this slogan a reality is massive. For the sake of equity to individuals and for the sake of cohesion in our society, this reality must be achieved. We should not accept the concept of a society with a large and permanent under-class, limited in their opportunities for work, for social participation and for individual fulfilment. Such concepts as Basic Education for All, as espoused by UNESCO, and High Quality Education and Training for All, as adopted by OECD, are part of the response of education to this situation.

There is a universal recognition that, for people to meet the changing demands in such diverse areas as employment, health, political participation and personal relationships, both a broad educational foundation, as implied by the above concepts, and also a continuing involvement with learning throughout life are required. The practical implementation of this recognition is a major issue-nationally and internationally-forcing a reconsideration of all aspects of education in the effort to meet this challenge. This reconsideration of the operation of education systems involves not only organizational and institutional redesign but also the very processes and purposes of education.

Higher education is, and will continue to be, a focal point for the changes affecting education, universally. In considering the future of higher education, a fundamental aspect must be its role in the education system as a whole and, specifically, its role in the reconceptualization of current aspects of education, to meet a challenge which is relevant to the good health of the whole society.

One of the most significant impacts on the role of higher education, and one which affects all other areas, has been the acceptance of the implications of 'lifelong learning', for so many years merely a slogan but now accepted as an appropriate response to the impact of change on human life. The Fifth International Conference on Adult Education (CONFINTEA-V) adopted the Agenda for the Future, which deals specifically with the role of higher education in this framework lifelong learning. It pointed out the growing demand for adult education and the necessary implication to open schools, colleges and universities to adult learners. In doing so, it challenges all these institutions to be prepared to adapt programmes and conditions, to develop ways of recognizing prior learning, to establish joint university/ community research and training partnerships, to involve adult learners in interdisciplinary research in adult education, to make this process of education for adults a systematic and continuing part of higher education.

The contributions of higher education may be usefully considered in terms of the follow-up meeting on Jomtien, held at Amman under the auspices of the

International Consultative Forum on Education for All, in June 1996. The assessment of that meeting was that great strides had been made in the six years since Jomtien, but that the targets for the decade would not be met without greater and more effective effort. Eight common concerns were identified for the meeting, arising from the seven regional policy review seminars held during a preparatory phase.

— the 'expanded vision of basic education' needs to be applied both in policy and practice;

— more resources must be found for basic education;

— the recruitment, training and status of teachers must be improved;

— the quality of education must be improved to enhance learning achievement;

— assessment of learning achievement must be generalized;

— more emphasis is still needed on girls' and women's education;

— basic education must be made more available to children, youth and adults with special needs; and

— more attention needs to be given to develop adults' numeracy and literacy skills and on sustaining these skills.

A number of these points relate to resources, and to the political and social will needed to sustain and increase current efforts. In these aspects, universities have no more to contribute than the rest of society, although in the effective use of resources a contribution may be made. For the other points, however, higher education has much to offer, and particularly in those dealing with teachers, with quality of education, with more generalized assessment, and with means of increasing access.

A major part of the proper contribution of universities to the system as a whole is intellectual: in analysis, evaluation, synthesis and reconceptualization. This is not an area in which higher education has a good recent record. In particular, research has played a much less significant role in education than in other social fields, such as medicine. The other area of contribution is in the preparation and continued education of people with special capabilities. A key aspect of both of these areas is in the improvement of the quality of education. In efforts to improve access and participation, it is often easy to forget that these are not enough on their own.

Conceptual contributions

Many recent approaches involve the idea of a core or common curriculum as a foundation, followed by a set of diverse pathways into higher and vocational concept of a common curriculum for all both adopt this approach, as do many of the nationally based initiatives, even in countries which formerly had little national involvement in this area.

In common curriculum learning is basic and essential. They are basic in that they are intended to provide a foundation or base on which subsequent or related learnings may be built. They are essential in the sense that they are intended to equip learners for a satisfying and effective participation in social and cultural life. Core curriculum theory has strong affinities with democratic ideology, and starts from the assumption that constructive and varied participation in social and cultural life is the right and responsibility of everybody.

The curriculum development involves highly complex processes. It includes political processes, as the various stakeholders in curriculum decide on their interests and negotiate to achieve maximal effect. It includes the development of curriculum materials and media planning related to presentation. It includes the key players, teachers and students, interacting to bring reality to plans and policies. It includes complex conceptualization in relation to the knowledge, understandings and competencies selected-and those excluded. It is in the conceptual development involved in curriculum change that universities should play a key part.

Given their central role in the development of new knowledge and the reappraisal of what exists, universities have much to contribute to the dialogue that is necessarily involved in curriculum changes. The final result at school level reflects many judgments, made on a number of different bases, as to what is excluded, what is included and how the latter is organized. Ideally, the best of scholarship should be involved in the assessment of the result of these decisions.

Given the major changes in all fields of knowledge-not merely addition but radical revision in many instances-a continuing dialogue is necessary between those who are involved in the redefinitions of the frontiers of knowledge and those entrusted with the task of interpretation at the school level. A major issue in this dialogue will be the willingness of both sides to understand the particular context of the other. In the past, constructive dialogue has been too rare and both sectors have been the worse for this failure. The fault does not lie on one side only and the remedy will require effort both from the universities and the schools.

Most universities have the necessary base disciplines to provide the foundation for such processes, but there will be a need to show that the people involved have developed them in ways which are sensitive to the particular context of schools and systems. It is increasingly obvious that the pace of change, which societies have found so disconcerting, will continue and that we must build better means, or adopt more useful processes, to help us cope with it. Universities provide an ideal setting for such studies which should take various forms. One necessary form is to follow up the long-term effects of current events-technological, economic or social.

A case in point is the 'greenhouse effect', where scientists and environmentalists have joined in a campaign to lower the emission of particular gases. These campaigns are not particularly popular and run the danger of exaggeration and being accused of scare-mongering. Yet, such thinking is necessary if we are to avoid or minimize the worst effects of our own way of living. To place such studies in a university environment should avoid the worst excesses and ensure appropriate safeguards. To carry out such studies demands a level of interdisciplinary co-operation that universities have often found difficult, and yet it is unlikely to occur elsewhere.

The gathering together of so many disciplines gives the universities a unique strength-provided they have the will to use it. A further form of study which would be of value is through more general speculation on forms of social change, together with a rigorous exploration of the implications for education systems. To a great extent, changes in education systems in recent years have come from adoptions of patterns from other areas of activity, in particular from business management. Such ideas as decentralization and re-engineering have been adopted uncritically into education systems, without the rigorous evaluation that such adaptations require.

Activities such as those we have discussed for higher education imply the need for the development of networks, in order to bring together the variety of strengths and specialisms required in such areas as future studies, system evaluations and curriculum development. Few universities on their own can have all the expertise required and, even where it exists, it may need support from elsewhere. The strengths in a particular university can, in combination with the quite different strengths of other universities, produce much more powerful results, within each partner and in the communities which they serve. It is a matter of real concern that current pressures on universities are placing them more in a competitive mode than a co-operative one.

Yet effective service for the community generally, in line with the best tradition of universities, implies a strong need for networks. The UNESCO chairs and the UNITWIN projects provide a good starting-point for such networks. Developing countries, in particular, have much to gain from this sort of approach, as they may radically increase their access to needed specializations without a corresponding increase in cost. UNESCO has also been successful in establishing regional networks of considerable power, and even greater potential, such as the Asia-Pacific Programme of Educational Innovation for

Development (APEID), a network of over 200 institutions in forty countries. Such initiatives offer considerable promise for future activity.

Within broad networks, such as APEID, there is scope for more specialized groupings, selected on the basis of common interest and of capacity to co-operate with, and contribute to, each other. The new information technologies dramatically increase the power of networks such as we have described. It is no longer a matter of increasing the impact of personal contact only through mail and telephone. The fax and e-mail provide an immediacy of contact and a wealth of available resources wherever they are available, and the spread is growing significantly. Virtual Conferences, i.e. conferences using computer links, have already been tried out to good effect and provide for a quite unprecedented range and variety of contacts which can revolutionize research possibilities.

Personal contributions

The most important thing universities do for the public sector is to train men and women adequately for the professions. In return for doing this, governments extend to academics in universities the freedom to do research. It is a relation with some tension in it. It is a bargain-struck between government, which has the money and which needs skilled professionals to service society, and universities, which have scholarship, science and knowledge which is the basis of good practice. It is an enlightened bargain because the most inspired learning occurs when the teacher is free to teach from his or her own enthusiasm and expertise. It is in professional preparation in general that the university role is so important, but we shall focus here on one area of professionalism in particular, the preparation of teachers, since here is the area which will impact most directly, and most fundamentally, on the extension and improvement of education in the schools.

Two major recent initiatives have stressed further the vital necessity to redirect attention to the preparation of teachers, if we are to achieve the lifts in quality which education currently requires. Many of the attempts to reform education in recent years have seemed to assume that teachers are irrelevant, or even hostile, to reform and have concentrated on structural matters, often leaving the classroom quite untouched, and thus failing to reach the heart of reform-the learning process itself. Without the active and effective co-operation-operation of teachers, the substantial improvement of the quality of education is not possible. The nine recommendation of the 1996 ICE are as follows:

1. Recruitment of teachers: attracting the most competent young people to teaching.
2. Pre-service training: a better linkage between pre-service training and the demands of an innovatory professional activity.
3. In-service training: both a right and a duty for all educational personnel.
4. The involvement of teachers and other agents in the process of transforming education: autonomy and responsibility.
5. Teachers and their partners in the educational process: education as a responsibility for all.
6. New information and communication technologies: serving to improve the quality of education for all.

7. Professionalization as a strategy for improving the status and working conditions of teachers.

8. Solidarity with teachers working in difficult situations.

9. Regional and international co-operation: an instrument to promote teacher mobility and competence

An essential area for concentration by the universities is in pre-service courses for teachers, for many of which they are directly responsible or on which they have a major potential impact. This is an area demanding close and fundamental attention, as there have not been the conceptual changes which the circumstances warrant. Yet, these courses depend to a degree on the quality of entrants and this has become a matter of concern in many countries where the academic quality of entrants has declined substantially in recent years. This, again, depends on the perceived status of teachers, frequently under threat as teachers are blamed for the problems encountered by education.

There is an obvious link also to teachers' working conditions which are often seen now as more demanding and less rewarding, both in prestige and money. A further link is with the new technologies, seen as offering so much promise of better learning but viewed with apprehension by many teachers, who lack the opportunity to become competent in this area. The complexity of the situation must not discourage universities from making the necessary intellectual investment to improve the preparation of teachers. Some considerable time has passed since there was a thorough reconsideration of the requirements of teaching, placing that reconsideration in the context of career-long education rather than with all the emphasis on the initial preparation.

The nine recommendations above from 1996 ICE may be appropriately applied also to universities. University emphases on the importance of teachers in other institutions also require a recognition of its importance within.

It is not only for teachers that higher education has a special responsibility, but for the variety of education specialists required at all levels and in all sectors of the education system. These include curriculum and assessment specialists, education technologists, reading advisers-the list can go on. What is common to this diversity is the need for careful and relevant preparation, recognizing that learning on the job is no longer sufficient. Nor is that approach-'learning on the job'-sufficient for those in leadership positions in education, including school principals.

The almost universal pattern of greater decentralization now places not merely more responsibility at the school level, but also quite different types of responsibility: not only for curriculum and pedagogy-the traditional areas-but financial management, industrial negotiation, team-building, personal counselling and career-planning, to mention only a few. Specialist principals centres are being developed in many countries, in association with universities, as a recognition of the need. This raises also the question of professional recognition of such roles in education, parallel in form perhaps to the specialist colleges in medicine. The whole field of adult and continuing education is one with which universities must come to terms, recognizing that the commitment to lifelong learning must be accepted as a basis for more integral links with this key sector and higher education.

The pace of change, both with respect to base knowledge but also in relation to social and ethical demands, requires all professionals to continue with their professional education. We now know much more, too, about the necessary characteristics of such education. These must not only reflect the principles of adult learning but recognize the unique context of particular areas of professional practice. It is healthy to see the involvement of professional bodies in such developments, through medical colleges and institutes of engineering, for example.

The universities still have an enduring place in such courses, to ensure a level of intellectual challenge and a continuing reappraisal of the professional processes. Professional certification and registration should not become cosy processes of self-justification, but subject to the rigorous procedures which should properly be the hallmark of universities. This is not to belittle the very necessary contribution of the professional bodies, but once again to assert the unique way in which universities can bring a wide range of disciplines to focus on a particular field of human endeavour.

Higher education is not always successful in doing this, but the capacity is there. CONFINTEA-V, with its stress on lifelong learning, raises again the role of higher education in a wider field of professional development, including all those educators, trainers and developers who have key roles in the framework of lifelong learning, not only in the teaching roles but also in the research and service roles. To do this implies not only a need for initiatives from within the universities, but also for them to be more ready to listen to the needs defined throughout the whole system-formal and informal. As part of this recognition, universities will need to make available to their own staff a relevant professional development on the same basis as is offered to other professional groups. A significant issue for universities in all its work in the preparation of professionals will be the education of girls and women.

2

Modernisation and Higher Education

Higher education institutions are complex systems which interact with the institutions around them, namely, with the existing political, economic, cultural and social systems. They are influenced by their local and national environment (or meso-environment) and, increasingly, by their regional and international environment (or macro-environment). But they in their turn can, and even must, influence these different environments. These different environments are in the throes of change. These changes are, of course, characterized by broad tendencies which were frequently mentioned at the preparatory conferences: globalization, internationalization, regionalization, democratization, the rise of mass demand for education, relocation, marginalization, fragmentation and the increasing use of technology.

An initial paradox concerns the existence of a powerful movement towards globalization of the economy through the setting up of multinational corporations and financial holding companies which are becoming increasingly sprawling and hard to control, side by side with a proliferation of small and medium-sized firms(SMFs) and even the growth of an informal economy which in some countries has supplanted a planned economy. On the one hand, an increasing number of business takeovers is occurring for financial more than economic reasons, involving job losses, increasingly numerous reorganizations on the basis of financial results and frequent changes in communication and personnel management policies.

Enormous sums of money circulate and can wreck the economy of a whole region. This is particularly true in the case of fragile emerging stock and money markets where capital moves unhindered and a few private individuals can upset the currencies of the countries of a whole region in a few days, and thus bring about chain-reaction bankruptcies, smash growth and create social Hiroshimas. This form of globalization tends to bring about a profound change from 'civilized capitalism' to 'unbridled capitalism'.

The civilized capitalism of the post-Second World War period has been built, at least in many countries, on firm foundations: full employment, a more egalitarian division of the fruits of labour, security of life and the satisfaction of collective needs, which have reached fairly high levels. Unbridled capitalism is built on the increasing powerlessness of states and even of international institutions to control the markets, to erect safety barriers, to combat greater and greater hidden unemployment and to counter the precarious situation of an increasing number of individuals, and an increasingly inegalitarian distribution of income within countries, as well as an ever more marked concentration of resources in the industrialized countries. On the other hand, over and against the large anonymous blocs, local initiatives based on improvization and designed to provide the wherewithal to live or survive are being established where the need exists. In many countries, nearly all technical and vocational training is developed in this informal context.

In the most developed countries a whole series of SMFs, many of them dependent on the multinationals through sub-contracting or franchise agreements, rise and fall. Others come into being as the result of a key idea or a newly acquired skill. For example, small venture-capital companies have been set up in the science parks around certain universities to develop new technologies stemming from scientific research. In addressing their employment problems, many states' awareness is growing that these SMFs are increasingly becoming reservoirs of employment, but they are aware, too, that their existence is very frail in the face of the large anonymous units on which they depend.

A second paradox connected with the first concerns a profound change in patterns of workforce migration when businesses relocate. While cheap labour migrated in the past to places where businesses were situated, the converse is now taking place; firms move to places where there is a supply of cheap labour. At the same time, highly trained professionals migrate towards relocated businesses, which strangely enough recruit few highly skilled local staff. The immobility of unskilled labour is encouraged by a large combination of factors. The first factor is primarily financial: when the same product costs \$24.8 in wages if it is manufactured in an industrialized country and \$0.28 in certain developing countries, few company managers subject to competition can afford to hesitate. The second factor is the current, increasingly drastic policy of closing the borders of the rich countries to numerous would-be migrants. This policy on the part of governments is particularly strengthened where extreme-right movements have become formidable and are seen as real dangers to democracy. The increasingly common phenomena of urban and school violence, ghettoes inhabited only by people leading a hand-to-mouth existence, long-term unemployment, the increasing number of refugees in all regions, the lack of prospects and growing feelings of insecurity all result in knee-jerk reactions of rejection and a tendency to close ranks.

However, this attempt to keep unskilled labour in one place goes together with increasing migration by the highly skilled labour produced by the most developed countries. Here again, several factors combine to favour this process. As they come in most cases from wealthy countries, the managers of relocated businesses prefer to place their trust in highly skilled labour trained by renowned higher education institutions, sharing as they do the same culture, values and language of international communication, and they tend to distrust local professionals regardless of their qualifications. Furthermore, experience of work in different places is regarded by them as an asset in terms of skills, adaptability and impartiality vis-à-vis local interests.

Distance itself is no longer much of a drawback as a result of improved air travel, reduced costs and the numerous possibilities held out by the new information and communication technologies (IT) of staying in touch with one's professional and family circle. Those who forecast that relocations would lead to an increased recruitment of highly qualified local executives trained by local universities have been wrong. National intellectuals trained in reputed foreign universities and adapted to that environment have had more opportunity to be recruited on the spot and transferred to other places. There is thus a brain drain from the developing countries either to places where planning and designing takes place - usually in wealthy countries - or to places of manufacture in other developing countries, with no true participation in the local communities and an increasing integration into a shifting, hermetically sealed international community. It is not sufficient for a developing country wishing to attract relocated firms to possess a supply of cheap labour. Numerous countries, many of them in sub-Saharan Africa, have had their offers rejected because of their supposed political instability and their low overall educational level in both quantitative and qualitative terms. A divide is thus also created between one developing country and another, and the gap is likely to widen with time.

A third paradox, which represents a genuine challenge, concerns the effects of demography. In the majority of developing countries we see runaway population growth whose effect is an increased demand for education; the public authorities are unable to find the necessary funds and are even compelled to reduce them still further as a result of a heavy public debt and structural-adjustment policies. In most of the wealthy countries, however, very low rates of population growth in recent years have gone together with ageing populations, increasingly lengthy full-time education and an ever later entry into working life.

The ageing of the population in the wealthy countries raises completely different problems. While there is also a very strong demand for education in those countries, this is due not to demographic factors but to a prolongation of education and a desire to raise the overall educational level. The extension of education is usually due to a twofold constraint: first the difficulty of finding a job without a minimum level of education; second, the resolve of governments to keep young people at school in order to reduce unemployment figures and to avoid pre-delinquency and even delinquency problems among young people left to their own devices, even if certain courses of study have a disguised child-minding role rather than an education and training function.

On the one hand, then, we have a mass of young people deprived of adolescence, forced to accept poor working conditions and ready to attempt the impossible in order to escape their situation. On the other, we have young people whose adolescence is prolonged, many of them with no prospects or future, full of energy which they cannot turn to good account because of their situation of long-term dependence; a not insignificant proportion of them seeks an outlet in artificial paradises (recent surveys indicate that in some countries one 12-year-old child in four has already dabbled in drugs). On one side, a hard life and a desire for possessions in order to live better in a poor environment; on the other, existential anguish and a desire to progress in order to find a more fulfilment in a wealthy environment.

A fourth paradox concerns the exponential development of scientific and technological knowledge, including the new information technology and the biotechnologies. As the result of increasingly fruitful scientific research, the new technologies hold out increasingly bright technical prospects for confronting the challenges of sustainable development. The regional conferences, however, showed that the countries most in need of them had difficulty in using them to solve their problems. The IT offer extraordinary possibilities: electronic mail, access to the most varied data bases, distance training, buying and selling, electronic money, virtual universities and virtual exchange networks.

The biotechnologies allow genetic manipulations that are capable of improving food production and combating some of the evils caused by pollution. Yet the gap between the developed and developing countries is widening rather than narrowing. harnessing this technology will require considerable investment in hardware, software and staff development'.

However there are many obstacles in the developing countries: 'The small existing number of potential users possessing both the capability and equipment to benefit from access to electronic information networks; the scarcity and expensiveness of equipment, software and information in comparison with the North; the lack of accessible telecommunications infrastructure; telecommunications monopolies together with over-regulation and high cost; the uncertainty of electricity supply in many countries; the lack of inter-regional networks and co-operation.

Over and beyond the purely technical and material aspects, one of the major conditions for introducing such facilities lies in the supplying of computers with suitable, meaningful and sufficiently good educational messages'.The proper use of biotechnology depends on a whole set of conditions which are far from being met in the developing countries; quite apart from the physical conditions, we should not underestimate the part played by ancestral folkways.

The United Nations Conference on Environment and Development held in Rio de Janeiro in 1992 put forward clear diagnoses, however, and was a focus of awareness made much of by the media. Five years later the prevailing feeling is that, rather than improving, the situation has further deteriorated for lack of a sufficiently proactive follow-up. A major source of hope for some, science and technology are perceived as enabling the challenges of the contemporary world to be met. Viewed with suspicion by others, they are regarded as causing more problems than they solve: misuse by parties hungry for power and domination (arms production) and wealth (pollution), (bio-) ethical problems of all kinds and an instrument of inequality well conveyed in the formula used at the Havana Consultation: 'Islands of modernity in an ocean of poverty'.

A fifth paradox concerns culture. A globalization and internationalization of culture is occurring. By contrast, there is a thirst, even a frenzy, to defend cultural, communal and linguistic identity. One of the most important vehicles of cultural globalization is indisputably communication by image, particularly television. The latter is omnipresent in the developed countries; in the developing countries it is making increasing headway among families of all classes and is often also watched by other people in the vicinity: serials acting as vehicles for values centred on wealth and easy money, beauty, violence, sex and leisure pursuits are closely followed and are having an increasing effect on mental attitudes.

Everything originating in Europe and America is automatically seen as better in the eyes of many young people: shoes or clothes of a brand seen on television are more attractive than the same articles manufactured locally. The same televised sequences are shown almost simultaneously throughout the world; the Gulf War was viewed live like a serial. Television is increasingly seen as powerfully influential. Taking advantage of liberalization, the major financial holding companies are therefore attempting to carry out sweeping takeovers with a view to becoming majority shareholders in the big television companies.

In this way, what some call a 'global village' and a 'one-idea system' is developing. Other factors have, of course, contributed to this globalization of culture: the extension of communication networks through the development of IT, the liberalization of air transport, the use of English as the language of communication in many fields and the major schemes for student, teacher and researcher exchanges. Yet at the same time a quest is in progress for anything that can help to give people a sense of identity. This is the reason behind the proliferation of local radio and television stations, the increased interest in local newspapers and mailshots, the support for policies of free expression for all, the renewal of community activities and initiatives to preserve community languages.

The changes shaking the world at the dawn of the twenty-first century are therefore complex and cannot be interpreted simplistically. As always during periods of transition, the effects of upheavals are paradoxical and difficult to control in the short term and pose challenges in the long term which may be summarized as follows: the challenge to struggle against all forms of divides (between continents, regions, communities, social classes, races, etc.) and to establish the conditions for harmonious, equitable and sustainable development.

If society is changing, higher education systems are necessarily changing too, and the paradoxes are no less numerous. Let us try to pinpoint the main paradoxes in order to build up a pertinent vision of the role of higher education as this century ends.

An initial paradox can be seen in the fact that, despite uncertainties about employment, higher education is increasingly becoming a mass phenomenon, contemporaneously with a relative drop in the resources - financial, material and human - devoted to it. Both in the highly developed and in the developing countries, the number of enrolments is rising steadily, and, what is more, in disciplines for which employment prospects are the worst. Recent international conferences have confirmed that the goal of universal access has become the general rule in the industrialized countries, where the enrolment rate of the age group most directly concerned (ages 17 to 23) is already reaching 30 to 80 per cent. Although the development of countries and regions would seem to imply training targeted at certain sectors and thus the promotion of certain disciplines not necessarily all of a university nature, students rush to enrol in the long general university courses still considered by many to be the most prestigious courses, a tendency often further encouraged by official civil service statutes and by regulations on recruitment and promotion mechanisms. In general, we can say that individual and social demand is the main driving force behind the universalization of access. Universal access tends to be the norm in most existing societies.

Although this expansion appears to imply a proportional increase in resources, states, and particularly those of developing countries, are proving increasingly unable to cope alone with the highly expensive development of higher education. In many countries the lecture halls are overcrowded, are not designed to accommodate so many students and do not deliver education in the right conditions. Staffing levels have not kept pace, and many establishments have been forced to reduce the number of sessions of practical work and even, in some cases, to abolish them.

The imbalance between higher education institutions in the developed countries and those in the developing countries has increased dramatically: in the former, all students are increasingly provided with an e-mail address and access to the Internet; in the latter, not even the majority of teachers have this facility.

Most higher education institutions in the developing countries find a very large share of their budget burdened by welfare costs (grants, canteens, accommodation, health care, etc) and have enormous difficulty in attending to the upkeep of facilities and renewing equipment in good time, and sometimes even in paying teachers'salaries. This expansion without any proportional increase in resources has been accompanied by a growing number of failures. Higher education thus finds itself in a dilemma: to provide training for the greatest number in order to increase the overall educational level, or to strengthen selection mechanisms at all stages of entry.

The second paradox therefore still concerns the problem of expansion. While this should permit more equitable access, what happens in many cases is a strengthening of exclusion mechanisms. Accepting a larger number should enable all those who have the ability and motivation (here we find the concept of 'merit' in its true sense) to enter higher education. It has to be stated that in many institutions this is not so. Thus, women, despite their increasing participation as students, are still under-represented in many institutions, and almost everywhere their numbers are grossly inadequate numbers in the scientific and technological subjects, at a time when unceasing emphasis is placed on the important role of women in development.

Higher education institutions fail to set a good example: teachers and decision-makers as a whole are still mostly men, mainly in certain regions of the world. Low-income families cannot afford higher studies for their children because of the rising cost of such studies and the difficulty experienced by states in investing further. Restrictions on access by ethnic or religious minorities are a further problem in certain places, as also are those suffered by refugees from conflicts on various continents.

A third paradox concerns the simultaneous presence of an immense need to raise the educational level in order to increase the development level and the increase in unemployment among graduates. Politicians and families in every country endeavour to raise educational levels. In highly developed countries, secondary education has become the general rule but, in addition, higher education has become a mandatory route for a majority of young people. In the developing countries, although the pattern is not quite the same, there is a desire to follow the same path, but the means are not available. Yet this desire is quite legitimate, since the connection between a country's overall educational level and its development level stands in no need of proof.

A very recent phenomenon must, however, also be noted, namely, worsening unemployment among an increasing number of higher education graduates. This particularly affects certain developing countries where a higher education diploma used to be regarded as a passport to immediate employment in the civil service. As the result of a drop in the demand for civil servants and of structural adjustment policies, this road has narrowed, creating more and more out-of-work graduates and also causing the best brains to leave the country. This is particularly serious when we know the cost to the state of training a graduate. It doubtless also reflects inadequate planning, just as it calls into question the relevance of the training provided when graduates are unable to find a job or create their own employment.

The fourth paradox can be stated succinctly: too much state intervention and not enough state. There is too much state intervention where the latter, realizing how much it is investing in higher education, seeks to control the use of its funds by imposing its own rules and interfering unwisely in curricula, in the recruitment of students and teachers (for example, pressure to accept a student or biased appointments and promotions), or in the allocation of resources, or by failing to observe its various commitments, including financial commitments, by the deadlines set and thus harming sound management. But there is also too little state intervention when the latter has omitted to set itself a clear development policy for the country having regard to the local, national, regional and international context, when there has been no real consultation between the political and academic authorities about the role to be played in development by the higher education institutions, when there is no long-term perspective and when management by the state is essentially conducted from day to day and in reaction to events, i.e. mainly with an eye to the short term, when electoral considerations take precedence over the long-term interests of the community and when education in practical terms is not a priority.

Situations admittedly vary greatly from one country to another. Moreover, higher education institutions sometimes tend to strengthen unhealthy imbalances between the state and themselves. This is the case when they tend to confuse academic freedom and absence of accountability, accountability and control, academic freedom and individualism. This raises the whole question of autonomy and accountability both within the institution itself and between the state and the institution. The question is far from straightforward where private institutions are involved, particularly in countries where these abound.

A fifth paradox concerns the openness, lack of openness or isolation of higher education institutions: the need for internationalization but also for contextualization.There has been a proliferation of university associations over the past few years:

— Association of African Universities,

— Association of Arab Universities,

— Association of Universities of Asia and the Pacific,

— Association of Commonwealth Universities,

— Association of European Universities,

— Association of Latin American Universities,

— Inter-American Organization for Higher Education.

Numerous NGOs have been associated with UNESCO higher education work. The UNESCO UNITWIN/Chairs Programme has been able, by rallying support, to involve over 750 higher education institutions in 82 countries through 290 chairs and 30 networks. Student and teacher exchange projects have been arranged nearly everywhere in the world on the initiative not only of UNESCO but also of the most varied organizations, e.g. the UNAMAZ (Association of Amazonian Universities) network set up in 1987 and strengthened following the United Nations Conference on Environment and Development in Rio, the Association of Universities of the Montevideo Group, the COLUMBUS/ALFA network linking Latin America and Europe, the MEDCAMPUS Programme establishing contacts between the various countries of the Mediterranean basin, the numerous European programmes such as ERASMUS, LINGUA, COMMETT, SOCRATES, TEMPUS, ESPRIT, BRITE, SPRINT and ECLAIR, the UMAP Programme for exchanges among Asian countries, the AUPELF/UREF networks, the TOKTEN and TALVEN Programmes, the ISA network bringing together universities of the Atlantic islands, etc.

This wealth of activities is the sign of a concern and need for internationalization resulting from numerous interacting factors:

— a knowledge explosion and the inability of any one institution to master all disciplines;

— research increasingly carried out in multidisciplinary teams and a need to concentrate the best specialists on a particular topic;

— competition in the various sectors both of education and of research and evaluation, leading to a greater quest for quality and thus an enhanced reputation;

— the necessity in certain sectors to have access to costly equipment and the resulting establishment of partnerships based on the complementarity of assets and skills;

— internationalization of the markets and a need to train students able to adapt to different environments.

Such international openness naturally raises many problems, such as the obligation to spell out the specifications of exchange programmes (aims, entrance requirements, content, assessment methods), to list the strong points of the institution to be proposed to the parties, to attempt to define comparable quality standards, and so on.

This internationalization effort has had many positive effects. Yet it is not without danger since internationalization, if misunderstood, could cause institutions to try to gloss over certain unique features or to align courses on those of richer countries or more powerful institutions, when one of higher education's tasks is to contribute to the development of its regional, national and even local context. Needs are far from being alike from one context to another. A paradox therefore arises inasmuch as internationalization and contextualization are both necessary. This is a challenge to be met, particularly at a time when the use of new technology can easily lead to one-way teaching in which students are viewed only as the end-products of a process.

A sixth paradox arises because while the majority of branches of IT originate in basic scientific research carried out in the universities and have been developed through research in the universities or in joint ventures with business, in practice they are still extremely under-utilized in teaching, which sticks to out-of-date traditions of imparting knowledge face to face irrespective of the ultimate purposes of the training. Here again we have a paradox: on the one hand openness to what is new, and on the other hand lack of openness, while noting that in this field, as in everything affecting the development of society, the big question continues to be the increasing gap between industrialized countries and the rest.

IT holds out remarkable possibilities of solving certain problems in higher education. Some concrete examples may be appropriate. In the past, training a future surgeon in micro-surgery of the ear involved a very heavy investment in staff and time, as the trainer was able to take only a small number of students into the operating theatre because of the limited field of vision; this meant a large number of sessions in order to cover a sufficient variety of cases.

Nowadays, highly miniaturized cameras are available which are inserted into the ear and allow the operation to be filmed on the spot. A large number of students can therefore take part in such operations either as they happen or in recorded form and under infinitely better learning conditions than before. The possibility of digitalizing such films and storing them on a computer allows them to be very widely distributed, especially to medical schools whose resources are limited or which wish to use those resources for other purposes.

Scientific magazines and books are very expensive, particularly for the developing countries the state of whose libraries often borders on the disastrous, and they suffer from the increasingly rapid obsolescence of the knowledge they contain. Because of the considerable progress made in data storage and the development of electronic networks, it is becoming possible to link all educational institutions to the computers they need, it being equally possible to devise schemes for distance learning and virtual universities. Teleconferences are becoming increasingly common in many countries and institutions.

However, in addition to a deliberate policy of furnishing the necessary means of access in a spirit of co-operation and solidarity, we have to be able to change mindsets and habits that make lecturing almost the exclusive method of teaching. Many universities have sunk enormous investment in multi-media equipment for their lecture halls and classrooms, but such equipment is often underutilized even where the visual aspect is semi-indispensable for teaching and even where personal interaction between student and subject of study object is more appropriate and less burdensome than listening to a lecture.

There are many possible reasons for this resistance: force of habit, lack of training, fear of making a mistake as distinct from the feeling of security induced by the routine of lecturing, and, in particular, rigid management of the lecturer's time in the short term. This last aspect is important: a lecture requires, or at least appears to require, much less preparation time; the use of multimedia, however, demands considerable effort and a long period of planning, and a completely different way of organizing teaching.

Viewed thus, the lecturer's work undergoes a radical change: from being someone who simply puts over a message he or she becomes a designer and manager of learning; in this way he confounds the saying that at university there is too much teaching and not enough learning. The role of the students, too, changes accordingly: they find themselves building up their knowledge and not simply absorbing it with a view to reproducing it as faithfully as possible. Here, higher education finds itself facing the need for a profound change.

A seventh paradox particularly concerns the universities and relates to their research task: the majority of teachers possess researcher status but, strange to say, there is much less actual research and even less 'contextualized' research in places where the need is greatest. Research is one of the three basic tasks of the universities; in most of them, nearly all teachers claim, and officially obtain, the status of researcher, which is not the case in other higher education institutions of an exclusively professionalist nature.

Today, the universities are found to have lost their monopoly on scientific, and even basic, research. The multinational corporations are increasingly establishing their own research centres and more and more SMEs specialize in research and development. An increasing number of universities have reacted positively by creating science parks in their vicinity which attract and group together specialized centres of this nature, allowing partnerships useful to both sides to be established. More and more small, joint-stock, research and development companies are appearing in these science parks, the shareholders being the university and the private sector, sometimes joined by local, national or regional public bodies.

Certain universities have acquired a strong reputation in the research field by following a relevant scientific policy or through a policy of attracting researchers from all over in the world. This encourages a brain drain at the expense of less wealthy universities - a brain drain also caused fairly often, it must be admitted, by inadequate pay and professional prospects and by the lack of freedom in many countries - and thus actually helps to widen the gap between certain regions of the world because insufficient researchers return. Side by side with those universities, however, there is a host of others where researcher status is merely a hollow word. The reasons are many and mutually reinforcing:

— too many supervisory or teaching tasks for young researchers during their most creative years;

— absence of proper laboratories with just the right amount of staff, equipment and logistic facilities in quantitative and qualitative terms;

— little or no supervision by senior local academics;

— a cruel lack of documentation or difficulty in gaining access to computers;

— absence of funding;

— need to seek a spare-time job in order to feed the family.

This situation is particularly common in the developing countries where, in addition, the requirements for 'contextualized' research involving both the social sciences and science and technology are especially numerous. Paradoxically such research is entrusted to foreign graduates who are not always aware of the particular needs of that environment and who demand large salaries and expenses, which sometimes leads to recurring costs that are not easily funded. This should make us reconsider certain co-operation policies.

The higher education institutions are in the throes of profound and complex change. Their contexts are extremely varied. The paradoxes are numerous. In the search for solutions it would be dangerous to ignore the various contradictions; choices cannot usually be expressed in terms of 'either this or that' but rather in terms of 'both this and that depending on the context', for visions and actions must be situated. Behind this plurality, however, lurk basic needs common to the whole of humanity. Thus, while visions and actions must be set in a context, they must be permeated above all else with a universal vision whose purpose is to bring about a more just and equitable society.

Higher Education: New Challenges

Traditionally, higher education has provided the wisdom and expertise which equip young people for their future roles as social leaders. This remains valid since higher education must uphold the education and values which mould socially responsible citizens. However, today, the role and profile of students in higher education has become extremely varied. In response to the reality of mass demand, the necessity to diversify has become a challenge for every country. Issues such as access, quality, relevance and internationalization are under closer scrutiny and students are insisting on greater dialogue between the partners involved so that they may select courses which permit them to accede to acceptable levels of employment, hence to social development.

Since students will be tomorrow's leaders, it is essential that their opinions be articulated and widely disseminated amongst all partners concerned with development. Without the support of young people who feel positive about the principles and modalities chosen to advance this process, its future could be gravely compromised. The student debates centred on three simple but basic questions -why young people were entering higher education, what they were learning and how this knowledge was being acquired. Their reflection revealed a number of profound concerns, the most urgent of which was the need to strike a correct balance between education and training. This relates not only to the content of their courses but also to the quality of their professors, to the capacity of systems and institutions to meet the educational needs of special groups, and, above all, to the social and personal values promoted during the learning process.

The student community showed itself to be fully aware of the main issues dominating this sector today and of their complexity. While they understood that solutions were not easy to define, they insisted that attention be paid to the discrepancy between their aspirations for their studies and the reality encountered. Moreover, the students readily acknowledged the reality of our knowledge-intensive society. It was noted that education policy-makers worldwide must rethink their approach to the new social order where the generation and availability of knowledge and know-how have undergone radical change. As well, the students recognized that knowledge has become a vital factor in the globalization process now taking place. Clearly, a top priority for any country is its access to global forces - i.e. those which shape societal change.

The generation and availability of knowledge, its applications and the institutions which foster these processes are at the cutting edge of this challenge.

Support was strong for the creation of a new educational vision which might orient the renovation of educational policy and, in turn, influence the character of systems and institutions. Also, content and methods will be renewed so as to provide the skilled human resources needed by specific communities. To attain these objectives, due and proper respect for the status of the professoriate is an essential factor. Unless this profession enjoys the full support of a given community or nation, it cannot contribute to the education and training processes in the optimal manner. In addition, the debates emphasized the potential to be derived from the internationalization of higher education. This phenomenon encourages contacts which help foster the human capacities to deal with cultural diversity which affects numerous aspects of social and economic development. However, for this to be successful, much depends on the willingness of partners to share their expertise and ensure its adaptation to different contexts.

One of the major traditional roles of higher education has been the education of social leaders. In the past, advanced study was the hallmark of the elite. Thus, a university degree equipped one for executive functions by virtue of its exclusiveness. Today, in this regard, the situation is very different, due to the massification of systems which renders a tertiary credential commonplace. Nevertheless, the need to educate and train citizens for their particular social era and its challenges remains valid. Moreover, at the end of the 20th century, there is a feeling of confusion and even of pessimism regarding the future direction of society and the ability of mankind to resolve grave social issues.

According to the UNESCO's report on *Education for the Twenty-first Century*, the four bases for action are:

learning to be, to do, to know and to live together. However, given global problems, these objectives are not easy to attain. Citizenship means, on one hand, possessing a sense of responsibility for one's local community and, on the other hand, understanding the wider socio-cultural context of the global village. To achieve this duality, contact, information and education are three crucial means of acquiring the attitudes needed to live and work in a world which is increasingly diverse and multicultural but where sharing and solidarity appear to be less supported.

The Human Development Report gives an annual picture of the indicators of progress: income, social inclusion, access to education and health services, living standards and poverty levels. Young people are usually disturbed by the inequalities of development and strive to remedy these through their choice of career and through their involvement in civil society. Today, citizenship is both national and international in ambit. It requires moral courage and clearly defined values which are lived daily and commitment to an understanding and tolerance of others.

Higher education can contribute very significantly to promoting citizenship through an international curriculum and the facilitation of academic mobility. Studies in fields such as the humanities, languages and international relations have much to contribute in this respect.

Higher education can never be reduced to mere training as its purposes and perspectives are too broad. Students have great expectations of their post-secondary studies and seek debate and exchange on a number of issues crucial to the development of their societies and of themselves as young adults. Hence, the tradition of this sector to produce educated and curious minds not only remains valid but must be the goal of all institutions, even in systems where provision is diversified. A new society will depend greatly - if not totally - on different attitudes and deeper understanding of difference.

It is also crucial to an analysis of higher education and its links to the world of work. Thus, it is inevitable that the various partners concerned with such questions must consider the consequences arising from current economic trends. These include a global shift towards deregulated economies and reduced government responsibility in matters related to social policy, new patterns of wealth which will surely influence at least the early years of the next century, and changing social attitudes to wealth as a public or private good. The ongoing volatility of the current economic climate has focused attention on the question of graduate employment. Depending on circumstances, this term can also cover the unemployment and under-employment of skilled people. For this reason, the issue must be studied in relation to the problems in the job market on a global scale.

Today, there is an estimated total of 35 million unemployed in OECD countries. Another 15 million are long-term unemployed or work only part-time. In the developing world, the Human Development Report, published by the UNDP, estimates that only 45% of the labour force has work -the vast majority in agriculture. Economists estimate that about 1 billion jobs (which is a virtually impossible target) need to be created as soon as possible to meet the global demand for employment. Young people -and especially those without education or training - are severely affected in such a climate. Moreover, even those with tertiary qualifications frequently experience difficulties in finding available or suitable career openings.

The availability of work and the security resulting from regular employment are certainly one primordial factor for sustained social and economic growth. Although these may be top priorities for citizens of all countries, they are proving elusive goals for too many governments which fear the long term consequences of unstable economic conditions. Against this background, the dialogue between the higher education community and its partners in the world of work has emerged as an urgent and essential tool in helping to tackle present economic questions.

In a changing world, education has become the essential passport to individual and social progress. In terms of sustainable human development, those without the necessary access to knowledge and know-how are at a distinct disadvantage and the gap in social and economic conditions between rich and poor countries is becoming alarmingly wider. Long term, such disparity will lead to more serious imbalances and even to situations of conflict. It is thus desirable to search for ways in which knowledge can be shared more equitably. In particular, advanced and complex knowledge must be adapted locally for the benefit of specific communities with respect for their own historical and cultural traditions. Thus, knowledge emerges as a rich and complex commodity embracing information, expertise and - most importantly - wisdom.

The successful production of good citizens and trained human resources is ample proof of a sound return on a nation's investment. However, in realistic terms, countries have limited resources for education and training. As a result, we see a closer link being forged between academic and other types of tertiary education. Such a trend is not without conflict because attitudes must change. Moreover, universities are being called to play a greater role in lifelong learning which, for many countries, has become a policy priority for ensuring the ongoing acquisition of skills which match the changing requirements of the job market.

If education is to meet the challenges of the future, it must be based on four foundations: learning to know, learning to do, learning to live together and learning to be. Furthermore, it urged countries to conceive education in a more encompassing manner and to be much less bound to the acquisition of knowledge solely through formal education systems. Therefore, as we approach the new millennium, the return on knowledge via education has become a sine qua non for basic social and economic advancement. Not only is this a fundamental human right and essential tool for the development process, but also it has emerged as one of the most effective means of shaping the globalization phenomenon so as to promote a more just social order and the attitudes of mutual understanding and co-operation required for a conflict-free society.

Issues in higher education

By now, the main issues in higher education are well known:

- increased demand in all countries leading to the massification of systems, thus challenging their quality and relevance;

— the resulting need to provide diversified teaching and training and institutional variety;

— reduced or static public resources for higher education so that costs are increasingly met by the main beneficiaries;

— the internationalization of higher education due to the academic and student mobility and to the generation and exchange of knowledge and know-how as a result of the Communication and Information Technologies (CITs);

— the need to address the impact of the globalized economy on higher education which involves very complex elements such as cost-sharing, co-awarded degrees and more effective strategies to handle the recognition of qualifications as the world's work force becomes more mobile.

Today, the higher education is undergoing major transformations. and the current issues must be seen in relation to the aims of the World Conference on Higher Education, namely:

— wider access to tertiary education on the basis of merit

— improved management and efficiency of systems and institutions

— closer links with the productive and economic sectors.

In a globally dependent world, it is often difficult for governments to arrive at local solutions which help resolve their own most pressing and specific problems. It is the responsibility of all sectors of the community to contribute to these solutions - in this respect, higher education, youth and employers have a key role to play in relation to their immediate national and regional environments. The achievement levels of individuals and nations, though varied, depend greatly on the elaboration of social policy which eliminates discrimination and exclusion and offers equal access to priority areas such as health care, education and employment. These are the central concerns of all nations today since they affect the lives of citizens in so many fundamental ways - one of the most important being their ability to realize their personal and professional aspirations.

Because of the overall positive return on investment in tertiary education and training, it is generally held that higher education offers people the opportunity to improve their lives to a significant extent. To do this, it must meet perceived needs in a given society and be seen inside a particular regional context. Overall, the basic problems facing national and institutional policy-makers are similar. Yet, their prioritization and solutions differ to a considerable degree because attendant socio-cultural and economic factors come into play.

Regional solutions to higher education issues must take account of the following specificities:

— in *Africa,* ongoing development problems including social stability, strong donor focus on basic education, and policies to ensure that higher learning is not marginalized;

— in *the Arab States,* the dynamic to modernize and expand systems and structures to cater for student demand in a context of cultural diversity, economic disparity and social volatility;

— in *Asia and the Pacific,* the need to balance the strong market forces driving higher education reform with the reiteration of the social and cultural factors shaping sustainable human development;

— in *Europe,* the quest for balance between the traditional prestige accorded to academic teaching and research and pressures to further strengthen the links between higher education and the labour market;

— in *Eastern and Central Europe,* the urgent renovation of higher education to meet both the political and social demands resulting from the transition to market economies;

— in *Latin America and the Caribbean,* more effective management of the steadily increasing investment in human capital, in both public and private systems, as the role of the region in the global economy continues to grow. In such an extremely diverse climate, a common commitment to the sharing of knowledge, resources and values emerges as a constant which can help guide all partners concerned with higher education towards mutually beneficial solutions.

Challenges for Professional Development

There is a significant shift towards the "user-pays" philosophy in all areas of social policy. With regard to higher education, students are now obliged to give much deeper thought to their choice of studies, and notably to the quality and relevance of these for the labour market. This should not, in any way, preclude the intrinsic value of higher education: both as the national and international resource which produces knowledgeable and broadly educated citizens whose understanding of a diverse and multicultural world can help foster better dialogue and understanding amongst nations; and as the source of advanced knowledge and know-how which are essential in a sophisticated socio-economic context. The main questions now at hand are different and quite new:

— firstly, are institutions playing their full role in educating and training graduates whose moral values and professional skills will contribute to an enhanced future social order in the 21st century - which was more implicit than explicit in the past?;

— secondly, and recognizing the current labour market volatility, are higher education systems and institutions giving direct consideration to the future employment prospects of their graduates - which was never (or rarely) necessary in the past?

The human resources issue must always be studied in relation to labour market trends where current questions include:

— the need for multi-skilled generalists, or for specifically skilled graduates who will become members of the workforce;

— the rise of contract labour;

— the impact of labour-saving technology;

— portfolio career paths;

— shorter working lives;

— the increased importance of lifelong learning for professional and personal development.

In industrialized nations, these trends result from strong advocacy for the market philosophy; in developing countries, the increased emphasis on structural adjustment is designed to stimulate their economic growth but is often is having a grave impact on their ability to ensure steady progress towards endogenous socio-economic and cultural development. While we see evidence of social reaction to this economic approach (notably by the election of governments with a commitment to a stronger state role and social agenda), the reality of the global economy suggests that this policy orientation will continue. In terms of higher education, these trends have provoked profound changes.

One of the key missions of higher education has traditionally been its role in and contribution to the world of work, because a nation's most highly skilled human capital has been taught and trained in this sector. In the past, manpower planning has regulated access to various areas of education and training so as to meet national requirements. However, today, when a degree or diploma in a particular field can be commonplace (and often over-subscribed), a number of new questions must be pondered:

— what are the consequences of a rapidly evolving labour market?

— what is the quantifiable and qualitative value of a skilled workforce?

— how should higher education systems and institutions diversify?

— what is the value of an advanced degree?

— what will be the typical student profile in the 21st century?

— how closely should higher education collaborate with the world of work insofar as curriculum and pedagogical innovations are concerned?

— what are the implications for the professoriate and for the academic career?

— how, in a changing world, do professions renew their contribution to the development process?

A number of suggestions have been advanced regarding the typical profile of the graduate in the new society of the 21st century. This person will have acquired:

— advanced knowledge - whether general or specialized in character;

— the ability to apply this to practical situations;

— a range of social or communication skills which will allow him or her to function in an increasing global world. These will include capacities in:

  — relationship-building

  — persuasion

  — self-management skills

  — leadership and co-ordination abilities

  — an adequate degree of business acumen

  — foreign language competence.

In addition, the graduate should demonstrate motivation and commitment to his or her chosen field as well as a high level of resilience and perseverance to meet the challenges involved. While this may be the desirable check-list, it is far from evident whether these capacities can be guaranteed by the education and training offered in each and every higher education institution for a number of valid reasons. These include not only a lack of financial and human resources to meet the increasing expectations and demands of students, but also the absence of vision which is necessary for that particular institution to operate in and contribute to the new society.

Amongst educationalists there is active debate as to what, exactly, this new paradigm should be. Some experts suggests that the educational process will move from:

— *teach*er-centred to resource-oriented learning

— group to individually-paced work

— closed to open systems without formal parameters

— provider-driven to user-centred curricula

— broad to selected provision to optimize relevance

— classroom to work and performance-based learning contexts

— isolated to networked environments

— one-way to interactive teaching

— national to global perspectives

— change-resistant to anticipatory educational management.

The inevitable process of change should be driven by the higher education sector itself. If this is not the case, then grave consequences could result as higher education will risk being shaped and manipulated by market forces which focus on short-term returns rather than long-term benefits. The UNESCO Policy Paper presents proposals for the pro-active institution which possesses all the attributes necessary for this challenging task because it:

— offers high quality training

— ensures entry on intellectual merit

— pursues knowledge

— shows commitment to social development

— offers lifelong learning opportunities

— links to the world of work

— engenders social debate and criticism

— provides advice and expertise for national decision-makers

— upholds academic freedom

— serves national, regional and international development needs.

There is a very clear and new emphasis on the role and responsibilities of the student community in this effort. Students are now the prime clients of higher education and, as such, their views merit full appropriate consideration when the relevance and quality of teaching, training and research are under scrutiny.

Successful higher education in the next century must open itself to a process of helping young people to better understand the world and be educationally empowered to contribute to society. The 1997 5th NGO Collective Consultation on Higher Education, debating the theme of *Graduate Employment*, identified four major challenges for this sector in the future:

— to ensure the education and training of creative graduates;

— to adapt systems and institutions to serve the labour market more effectively since employment has emerged as the new key concern for the student community;

— to promote radical innovation in the educational process so as to produce the new graduate profiles needed in a changing world;

— to forge new partnerships amongst the main stakeholders in higher education.

To achieve this transformation, a whole range of issues will require close scrutiny: for instance, institutional profiling, anticipatory leadership and management, constant innovation in teaching, training and research capacities, the provision of essential services such as career counselling, graduate placement and tracer studies, structures to ensure gender equity, recognition of cultural diversity and the inclusion of marginalized social *groups*, etc.

In this changing world, it is important to listen to the opinions of students concerning the future directions of higher education. This must be a priority aim which is realized through effective strategies and will result in enhanced student participation in the renewal process.

This objective is particularly important given the present paradoxical social climate where: on one hand, the enhanced level of knowledge, know-how and skills amongst graduates should stand them in good stead for the profound social and economic changes ahead;. on the other hand, they are faced with great uncertainties which prevent them from realizing their aspirations and fulfilling the potential of their qualifications. With regard to higher education in the next century, this sector must aim to:

— *be open to a* process of helping young people to better understand the world and be educationally empowered to contribute to society;

— help promote social values which privilege justice, equity and tolerance;

— become both increasingly international and more community based;

— continue to act as a principal forum for thought and discussion;

— recognize the validity of the student voice in the reform debate;

— actively involve student organizations in the reform process of systems and institutions.

In this chanign world, essential strategies to renovate the existing key educational tools include continuously updating of the curriculum, interactive teaching, career counselling, dialogue with employers and opportunities for interface between studies and work experience, contacts with peers from different cultural backgrounds, initial training and adequate provision for lifelong learning. Such strategies clearly acknowledge that students are amongst the main stakeholders in higher education and that they possess the *vision, the responsibility, the intelligence, the skills and the conviction* to be full partners in the future of this domain.

3

Higher Education and Human Development

Higher education is facing increasingly formidable challenges. To cope-up with the the needs of tody's information society the higher education systems have to be developed much broader than the concept of the traditional research university allows. The differentiation of the system of higher education is already an important trend in many countries, if not even a fact in some. But it will become universal, because higher education around the world will have to cater for increasingly heterogeneous groups of students.

Higher education institutions will.have to differ in the ways and degrees in which they combine teaching, training and research, transfer innovations and innovative thoughts into applications and to society as well as in the ways in which they stimulate their students to study, to search for knowledge. Therefore, they will differ in the content and structure of their programmes and the ways in which these are delivered, as well as the preparation and the profile of their teaching staff: their educators and tutors. Together these institutions, in whatever form and combination, often explicable only by culturally diverse historical processes, will have to provide the broad spectre of study facilities that can cater for an increasingly differentiated demand.

What, however, will not change is the necessity that these institutions will have to prepare new generations for the future. A future that, nowadays, is quickly and vastly changing like never before. Such a perspective should, however, not be seen as frightening, but as a challenge instead. It is a time for change to enter a new stage of humankind in which many of the ambitions on peace and progress of people around the world as these were laid down in the Charter of the United Nations, could be realized, if the opportunities are taken well. To prepare new generations for such a challenge, to empower them to make a difference, is an exciting task for all who are directly involved in or concerned with higher education today.

At both the international and national levels, fundamental forces are reshaping patterns of social organization, structures of opportunities and constraints, objects of aspiration, and sources of fear. Globalization envelops the world even as fragmentation and the assertion of differences are on the rise. Zones of peace expand while outbursts of horrific violence intensify; unprecedented wealth is being created but large pockets of poverty remain endemic; the will of the people and their integral rights are increasingly both celebrated and violated; science and technology enhance human life at the same time as their by-products threaten planetary life-support systems.

The concept of human development and the related concept of human security have, however, gained widespread interest and acclaim since UNDP's trail-blazing Human Development Report was first published in 1993. Indeed, important changes have taken place in the period of time in between. In particular the end of the era of super-power rivalry and military confrontation has unleashed an unprecedented number and variety of international transformation processes of economic and political, but also of social and cultural nature.

Globalization, introduced as an economic concept, has now become understood in a much broader sense as a forceful, overarching process that, indeed, penetrates into all different aspects of life and society. It offers great opportunities for sustained welfare and well being, but poses also numerous policy challenges. Those are related to the inherent risks created by financial markets lacking critical regulatory safeguards, as well as by a lack of or inadequate understanding of long-term development and interests of humans/people.

Both, in developing as well as developed countries, it has become fully clear that the state, although not a creator of wealth itself, has critical roles to play in providing an enabling environment for sustainable development. The 1997 World Development Report of the World Bank shows clearly how crucial an effective "State" is in this regard. It is becoming, however, an ever more complex task to find an appropriate balance, in particular, where civil society is weak and transnational forces overpowering. One of the crucial roles the "State" has to play is to ensure human security on the local, national and - in cooperation - within regional associations and the United Nations on the regional and global levels.

To ensure human security without which sustainable human development will not be possible. Our sustainable future will depend strongly on the ways in which we successfully can link up the spheres of daily life at the individual and local level and that of economic life on the regional and global level. This is particularly true in a time in which a remarkable revolution in information and communication technology permits high volume and high quality real-time voice and data transmissions.

Sustainable human development, however, is not only based on economy, organization and communication. Fundamental to a sustainable future is to ensure the proper use and stewardship of the heritage that was given to humankind in the form of the earth. This earth does not only provide us with the firm ground we live on and the natural resources we use in a great variety of production and consumption processes, but also the air we breathe and the water we drink. More than anything else our common earth represents a public interest and shared responsibility. Shared not only here or at a specific place, as water and air move freely - shared also, not only now or in a specific time period, as what we use now - in particular of depletable resources - will not be available for future generations.

As a consequence of its multi-dimensional character, sustainable development has been variously defined and described. The concept was for the first time indicated in Principle 1 of the Stockholm Declaration on the Human Environment:

> .... "Man has the fundamental right to freedom, equality and adequate conditions of life, in an environment of a quality that permits a life of dignity and well-being, and he bears a solemn

> responsibility to protect and improve the environment of present and future generations."

The Rio Declaration on Environment and Development in the Principles 1 and 3 stated in the same line, stressing more the right to development:

> ......"Human beings are at the centre of concerns for sustainable development. They are entitled to a healthy and productive life in harmony with nature." ......"The right to development must be fulfilled so as to equitably meet developmental and environmental needs of present and future generations."

These formulations link clearly human rights and environmental protection recognizing human rights as a fundamental goal and environmental protection as an essential means to achieve the "adequate conditions" for a "life of dignity and well-being" that are guaranteed. The links between human rights and the environment may be viewed deriving from the fact that human health and existence, legally protected as the right to health and the right to life, are dependent upon environmental conditions.

The concept of sustainable development was launched in 1987 by the report of the World Commission on Environment and Development (the "Brundtland Report"). There it was defined as: "meeting the needs of the present without compromising the ability of future generations to meet their own needs" and as "a process of change in which the exploitation of resources, the direction of investments, the orientation of technological development, and institutional change are all in harmony and enhance both current and future potential to meet human needs and aspirations." Sustainable development is not a fixed notion, but rather a process of change in the relationships between social, economic and natural systems and processes. UNESCO continues in the publication mentioned above as follows :.

> .... "Perhaps the most widely used definitions focus on the relationship between social development and economic opportunity, on the one hand, and the requirements of the environment on the other: i.e., on improving the quality of life for all, especially of the poor and deprived, within the carrying capacity of supporting eco-systems. This does not necessarily set fixed limits on "development," but rather recognizes that the prevailing notions and definitions of development must themselves evolve in relation to changing requirements and possibilities. .... sustainability calls for a dynamic balance among many factors, including the social, cultural and economic requirements of humankind and the imperative need to safeguard the natural environment of which humanity is a part. What is sought is the condition of "human security" for all people."....

The transformation processes indicated in the foregoing paragraphs, have intensified the global environmental interdependencies. Hence, the importance of the Agenda 21 process, officially started at the UNCED in Rio de Janeiro in 1992. There the international community endorsed the concept of sustainable development as the key to reconcile economic and social progress, while safeguarding the planet's ecosystems.

The intense public interest in the recent Kyoto Conference (1997) of the Parties to the United Nations Framework Convention on Climate Change provided a good illustration of the widespread support for sustainable development. The progress since Rio, however, has been disappointing so far; with a few exceptions like the initiatives to implement the Local Agenda 21. The discussions in Kyoto also illustrated that there exists still much uncertainty as to what actions exactly will have to be taken, to which levels we will have to rise to meet the challenges posed to us and also how to share common responsibilities in a just manner. It is here that there is a major responsibility for universities, indeed all the institutions of higher education, preparing new generations for a sustainable future.

Role of Universities in Human Development

Universities have a unique contribution to make, a contribution implicit and utterly in keeping with their mission of advancing learning through research and teaching. At the heart of any effort to understand and promote sustainable development are four key elements:

— the serious and pressing nature of the problem;

— the inter-/transdisciplinary scope of potential solutions;

— the international scale of their impact; and.

— the ethical imperatives of self-knowledge, self-discipline, moderation, fairness and justice for all

This unique contribution, however, is not self-evident. Specific action plans will be required, when universities are prepared to play this leading role. The *Draft Action*

Plan for Individual Universities of IAU , e.g., states that to this end each university, in its own action plan, should strive:

— to make an institutional commitment to the principle and practice of sustainable development within the academic milieu and to communicate the commitment to its students, its employees and to the public at large;

— to promote sustainable consumption practices in its own operations;

— to develop the capacities of its academic staff to teach environmental literacy;

— to encourage among both staff and students an environmental perspective, whatever the field of study;

— to utilize the intellectual resources of the university to build strong environmental education programmes;

— to encourage interdisciplinary and collaborative research programmes related to sustainable development as part of the institution's central mission and to overcome traditional barriers between disciplines and departments;

— to emphasize the ethical obligations of the immediate university community - current students, faculty and staff

— to understand and defeat the forces that lead to environmental degradation, North-South disparities, and inter-generational inequities;

— to work at ways that will help its academic community, and the graduates, friends and governments that support it, to accept these ethical obligations;

- to promote interdisciplinary networks of environmental experts at the local, national and international level in order to disseminate knowledge and to collaborate on common environmental projects in both research and education;
- to promote the mobility of staff and students as essential to the free trade of knowledge;
- to forge partnerships with other sectors of society in transferring innovative and appropriate technologies that can benefit and enhance sustainable development practices.

To become really successful and become true intellectual powerhouses in this field, universities will have to pay specific attention to the *internal drive* in university life of students and staff; of teachers, tutors and researchers.

Universities are in the first place centres of knowledge – not training schools, but places of critical thinking and scientific development. That is what justifies their teaching offer. And science is not motionless, a kind of pool of accepted ideas academics can draw from to provide a consensual lesson for the world to act on environmental matters. There is *no consensus* – neither in scientific nor in political terms. This is not due to a lack of debates but, more so to the *inner drive* of science development that cannot be planned and organized. Hence, the ups and downs of the *climate debate*, for instance. However, the facts are firmly on the table and sufficiently clear to choose for a cautious course.

Conviction needed to move on from the stages of *knowing* (savoir) and *being able* (pouvoir) to the stages of *wanting* (vouloir) and *daring* (oser)....to act. True leadership is wanted here to move in the direction of active participation in bringing about the desired changes: to encourage inter-disciplinary and collaborative research and education programmes; to promote inter-disciplinary networks of environmental experts at the local, national and international level;.to encourage among both staff and students an *environmental perspective whatever the field of study*;.to emphasize the ethical obligations.

Universities have become increasingly aware of the role they do have to play in preparing new generations for a sustainable future. Increasingly after Rio's Earth Summit, they tried to define and also to implement their roles in education for a sustainable future. To this end, they have at different times and places drafted and adopted ambitious declarations in which they have formulated the major principles and aims for the reform process into which they are prepared to engage themselves. A few early examples are the:

— Talloires Declaration of University Leaders for a Sustainable Future (1990 at Tufts University);.

— Halifax Declaration (IAU – UNU – AUCC, together with 20 university presidents from among others, Brazil, Indonesia and Zimbabwe, 1991);.

— Kyoto Declaration on Sustainable Development of the International Association of Universities (IAU, 1993);.

— University Charter for Sustainable Development (CRE-Copernicus, 1993).

Indeed, universities are increasingly called upon to play a leading role in developing an inter-/trans-/ disciplinary and ethically-oriented form of education in order to devise solutions for the problems linked with sustainable development. They must, therefore, commit themselves to an on-going process of informing, educating, and mobilizing all the relevant parts of society concerning the consequences of ecological degradation, including its impact on global development and the conditions needed to ensure a sustainable and just world.

Among all institutions of higher education there exists a strong feeling of responsibility with regard to their role in preparing new generations for a sustainable future. More than 200 universities from 42 countries are now members of the Talloires Group; almost 250 signed the CRE-Copernicus Charter. Of course, their arguments for this are also very pragmatic: at no time in history has there been a greater need for a well-educated, skilled and motivated work force, community and citizens. This is true for two reasons:

(1) the highly competitive nature of today's global economy, and most importantly,

(2) the growing realization that economic progress, both in developed and developing countries, must be based on the principles of sustainable development.

The universities involved share the conviction that economic progress and environmental protection are irrevocably linked. The one cannot be had without the other. One way to assure that this relationship is understood could be by incorporating environmental issues into the general education system - both in formal education and in corporate training programmes. In this context, it is unhelpful to think of environmental education as a separate category - the true world need is for better basic education. In fact the need for general environmental scientists is limited.

The conferences of the Association of University Departments of Environmental Studies (auDes) have made quite clear that we will probably need more the different environmental specialists in, among others, environmental law, resource economics, environmental chemistry, environmental medicine, toxicology and engineering. A good illustration here is the need to prepare future medical doctors to inform and teach the public on questions of environmental consequences.

Probably, the most important contribution of environmental scientists could be in the *"greening"* of curricula, by which in disciplinary curricula due attention is given to related environmental aspects. The most urgent need is to set good examples in ongoing activities. Starting with *"greening the campus"* and particularly focussing also on setting good examples in the practicals and research laboratories as well as paying due attention to choosing research topics and methods.

In line with their growing conviction that economic progress and environmental protection are irrevocably linked, the universities gradually shifted their focus from the environment to sustainable (human) development. They paid, among others, specific attention to the need of direct transfer of knowledge to developing countries. This is also the orientation that has been chosen by the World Commission on Sustainable Development, while preparing a work programme, which has to *"refine the concept and key messages of education for sustainable development"* and in so doing to integrate environmental, demographic, economic, social and a range of other concerns inherent in the complex notion of sustainability. This work programme.outlines the priorities for action by the United Nations system, and by UNESCO in particular as the specialized agency in the UN system for education and science and as a "task manager" for Principle 36 of Agenda 21, as well as by governments, NGOs, including organizations in higher education, major groups and the private sector.

Since the Rio Earth Summit, a new international consensus has emerged concerning the critical role of education in achieving sustainable development. Principle 36, one of the forty Principles in Agenda 21, concerns *"promoting education, public awareness and training"*, while in Rio there was unanimous agreement among developed and developing countries alike that education is *"critical for promoting sustainable development and increasing the capacity of the people to address environment and development issues."* The scope of Principle 36 is extremely broad, ranging from formal education systems at all levels, vocational training and development of the workforce to education in agriculture and health care, adult education and communication about environment and development.

Principle 36 also emphasizes that basic education is a prerequisite to environmental and development education, and remains a priority for many countries of the world, linked to the overall effort to combat poverty. Principle 36 is divided into three "programme" areas:

— Reorienting education towards sustainable development;

— Increasing public awareness; and

— Promoting training.

It is a "cross sectoral" principle and therefore seen as linked to virtually all other areas of Agenda 21.

At the heart of the new international consensus is a new vision of education and public awareness as the essential underpinning for sustainable development, a linchpin to support advances in other spheres, such as science, technology, legislation and production.

Education is being redesigned in terms of how to prepare people for life: job security and employability, the demands of a rapidly changing society, technological changes that now directly or indirectly affect every part of life; and, ultimately, the quest for happiness, well-being and quality of life. Education is therefore being redefined as a lifelong process that needs to be not merely readjusted, but restructured and reformed according to new requirements.

The World Conference on Higher Education is designed to develop the *"Vision and Actions"* needed to support this process. One of the requirements is the goal of sustainable development, an overarching concept that has broad implications for curricula at all levels of education. The thematic debate *"Preparing for a Sustainable Future: Higher Education and Sustainable Human Development"* tries to identify the visions and actions needed to ensure improved performance of Higher Education in this field. In doing this, it should contribute to the work programme of the Commission on Sustainable Development .

Evaluation five years after the Rio Earth Summit in the United Nations (1997) of accomplishments in the field of Agenda 21 was not favourable. Certainly, the universities have not done better. Good intentions and elaborated visions may not have been lacking, but the implementation in an unruly reality has proved to be difficult.

Two years after almost 250 universities signed the University Charter for Sustainable Development, few European universities could show real progress in the implementation. In his contribution to the IAU 4th Mid-term Conference Carl Einar Stålvant, CRE-Copernicus co-ordinator, titled *"Universities as actors in sustainable development"* comes also to the conclusion that many universities seem not to have lived up to the levels of their ambitions. The *"inner drive"* to contribute among staff and students in daily university life seems not yet strong enough. From the student side, however, this might already be changing.

The establishment of the Global Organization of Students for Environmental Action (GOSEA) is an encouraging sign. Stålvant is disregarding the limited success thus far, convinced that the Charter provides a focal point for university activities in the midst of a large amount of other activities and that it is this what makes the charter useful. To support his view, he listed a series of institutional mechanisms that have been put in place in recent years and hold the promise of more effective actions in the near future in the field of environmental care and housekeeping.

In Barcelona University, e.g. a vice-rector has been assigned to perform this wide-ranging task. Sincere engagement of the university leadership is essential. In many cases, however, true commitment and continuity and consistency in actions on the part of the students have also proved to be effective. Often, however, the increasingly larger numbers of students, the teaching "load", financial problems, lack of time and adequate facilities are given as arguments why actions were postponed. Others blame the lack of strong competition between universities, the governance structure of universities, the overly strong disciplinary character and ill-fated academic reward-system for the lack of action.

Against the aforementioned background it seems appropriate to focus on a thematic debate on highree education and sustainable development not so much on visions: these do already exist, even quite elaborate ones. There is much more need to focus on the reality, the difficulties in implementing all the beautiful ideas. One of the difficulties being that research has not yet produced all the required technical, economic and social solutions for the implementation of ideas and ideals. The discussion could therefore focus on:

— how to bring environmental concerns and hopes in a more sound relation.with the concerns and hopes regarding human development?

— what are the most important reasons for the slow and often lacking implementation of the well-developed visions in this area?.

— in which ways and with what kind of instruments could the process of implementation be energized and the "inner drive" strengthened?.

— how could the interaction between higher education institutions and society-at-large be strengthened to promote more forcefully the desired sustainable human development?.

The first question focusses on a balanced integration of ecological, technological, economic and socio-cultural components of sustainable development. To develop the argument and to see how this could be implemented in curricula and research, a world conference is particularly appropriate as it will ask for contributions from, among others, developed and developing countries as well as from countries in the transition phase.

The second and third questions are strongly related and are based upon the underlying questions: How can we stimulate universities to re-design their education and research *"to deliver green graduates"* in the same way we asked the private and public sectors to improve their products and policy some two decades ago?.How can we stimulate the private and public sectors as employers to require certain knowledge and skills of graduates to green their products and services, what will challenge students and universities?.How can we stimulate that *"green universities"* will more and more directly profit from their investments?.Having answered these questions, universities should address topics like:

— How can inter-disciplinarity be developed and encouraged?

— How can (theoretical) knowledge be better linked to its (potential) practical applications?.

— What changes will be necessary in higher education programmes and institutions to prepare future generations better for complex situations and problems, including ethical dilemmas?

— How can cooperation between national, regional and international (global) institutions in the field of sustainable human development be promoted so as to increase understanding for different positions and to become more effective?

The last question focusses on the relations of higher education institutions with the outside world. In the different university declarations mentioned, three aspects are stressed: - the relations with alumni and others in a world where employability and life-long learning are basics;

— the relations with governments and others in their enabling roles: to create the conditions under which the universities can perform their tasks well;

— the relations with different partners in various sectors of society which will help to shape shared responsibilities and cooperation in matters related to sustainable human development; in particular on the local and regional levels.

Since the UN Commission on Sustainable Development (CSD) adopted the Work Programme on Education, Public Awareness and Training, much work has been done to refine the concept and key messages of education for sustainable development. In particular, UNESCO has contributed as task manager for Chapter 36 of Agenda 21 through its Transdisciplinary Project "*Educating for a Sustainable Future.*" The development of ideas resulted eventually in the preparatory document "*Educating for a Sustainable Future – A Transdisciplinary Vision for Concerted Action.*" In these texts, the CSD explicitly calls upon the World Conference on Higher Education:

— to address the challenge of how to promote and strengthen an interdisciplinary approach in university curricula and research agendas for a sustainable future and to consider the further adaptation of higher education systems, as appropriate in this regard

— to give due consideration to how the reform of higher education systems may support sustainable development.

Innovative programs and projects from all sources, such as various major groups, including industries, women, youth and NGOs, should be encouraged and included in this inventory; encouraged the development and strengthening of international and regional alliances, associations and networks among universities and other educational and training institutions and professional bodies in all countries, in particular between those in developing and developed countries. These alliances should include distance learning, training for trainers, exchanges and mentoring; and stressed the need to improve the processes of generating, sharing and utilizing science for sustainable development and for more action-oriented, interdisciplinary research with greater focus on prevention and early identification of emerging problems and opportunities.

Many of the recommendations are clearly focussing on cooperation, creating synergy and exchanging information. These can be implemented in a balanced and pragmatic action plan. The challenge of how to promote and strengthen an interdisciplinary approach in university curricula and research agendas for a sustainable future, however, is of a different nature. So is the need to improve the processes of generating, sharing and utilizing science for sustainable development and for more action-oriented interdisciplinary research with greater focus on prevention and early identification of emerging problems and opportunities, as well as the necessity to carefully redesign effective processes of knowledge-sharing between universities, schools, NGOs, public institutions and enterprises in developed and developing countries.

Reorienting education to sustainability requires recognizing that traditional compartments and categories can no longer remain in isolation from each other and that we must work increasingly at the interface of disciplines in order to address the complex problems of today's world. This is true both within education where interdisciplinarity is slowly and with difficulty gaining ground, and between the spheres of education, work and leisure as life-long learning emerges as a key concept for planning and developing educational systems. It is also true as concerns the most important boundary of all: that separating those included in education systems from those who are excluded from them. Ultimately, sustainable development will require an education that not only continues throughout life, but is also as broad as life itself, an education that serves all people, draws upon all domains of knowledge and seeks to integrate learning into all of life's major activities.

As concerns sustainable development specifically, it is impossible to predict with reliability what will be the key issues on which people will need information in five, ten, twenty or fifty years. It is predictable, however, that such developments will not fit neatly into the existing and artificial sub-divisions of knowledge, which have been in place for more than a century. Hence, understanding and solving complex problems is likely to require intensified cooperation among scientific fields as well as between the pure sciences and the social sciences. Re-orienting education to sustainable development will, in short, require important, even dramatic changes, in nearly all areas.

The changes in nearly all areas will be dramatic indeed. The crucial question, however, will be whether an adaptation or even reform of higher education systems will be necessary to support sustainable development, to accommodate these dramatic changes.

This is questionable for two reasons: Higher education systems are quite different from country to country and have changed over time in the last century quite a lot. It is often the great differences from country to country and institution to institution that make international cooperation at the university-level so difficult. We do not know what questions and problems we will have to solve even in the near future and which combinations of expertise will prove to be the most fruitful.

Besides, aspects of sustainable development will be important in all different fields of knowledge, as "sustainable development will require education as broad as life itself.".The problem is not in the systems or structures, but in the way people operate. The change has to come from the minds of the people, their inner drive. They have to be ready to cooperate in very flexible ways over disciplinary and institutional boundaries. We must realize the slow evolution of the idea of specialization: a true specialist is often someone whose mind, because of the precision and richness of its knowledge can constantly open out onto other fields and know-how to put his own scholarship to work in training and to link it to all forms of knowledge. This does not mean that no changes at the system-level will occur. These will occur like before. These are, however, neither necessary nor in themselves sufficient to bring out the necessary dramatic changes. The action plan should instead aim more at actions that will not miss their impact on the *inner drive* of people.

Universities Role in Regional Development

While universities are located in regions, questions are being asked about what contribution they make to the development of those regions. Whilst it might be possible to identify passive impacts of universities in terms of direct and indirect employment, how can the resources of universities be mobilised to actively contribute to the development process? These questions are posed because development has a strong territorial dimension - national objectives can only be achieved by realising the full potential of constituent sub-national units and in this regard universities in different regions are being required to make a contribution. An obvious starting for an improved understanding can be provided by an audit of existing regionally relevant activities with the audit being jointly commissioned by universities and regional agencies.

Given the diversity of universities within a national territory, it would be also desirable if such an audit were co-sponsored by central government, in collaboration with a body representing the university sector as a whole. The starting point of any audit would be a direct economic impact analysis of universities as an economic sector. Universities are major employers of relatively high grade staff with considerable local spending power. While many of these staff may not be recruited within the region, support staff will be. The student body itself will also have a direct local impact through local purchasing. Students will be a net addition to the regional economy, insofar as they are recruited from outside the area. All of these impacts are readily measurable by conventional economic multiply analysis.

Likewise the effect on the overall employment structure of each region can be readily assessed by setting higher education in the context of the overall regional profile. This might reveal university employment growing whilst other sectors (e.g. agriculture and manufacturing) may be declining. These direct employment impacts are essentially static. More significant are the dynamic effects which a university can have through interaction with industry. These are more difficult to measure but a university can audit the geography of its industrial interactions by identifying the location of partners in research grants and contracts, consultancy, exchanges of research staff and spin-out of university companies.

Because such research based activity is essentially global in character only a small part is likely to have a regional relevance. A more significant impact is likely to be through teaching and the recruitment of graduates by regional businesses and through programmes of continuing professional development. Here it is possible to monitor the flow of students from home origins through different courses into local employment opportunities. The final area that an audit should cover is the contribution of universities to social and community development.

In many countries there are long established regional and local variations in participation in higher education and in the skills of the local workforce. Data on the flow of students through universities can also be used to identify the contribution of universities to raising levels of education attainment in different parts of the country and to enhancing skill levels of the workforce by recruiting non-local students and placing them with local employers. Vocational programmes in such areas as medicine and social sciences, which bring direct community benefits, can be identified. In addition to programmes targeted to the needs of employers, universities will need to demonstrate contributions to non-vocational education and cultural programmes in the Arts.

The role of the university staff and students in providing significant local audiences for the regional arts will need to be defined. The role of university staff and students in providing key leaders in local civil society by participating in voluntary activities, interpreting world affairs in the regional media and undertaking strategic analysis of the regional economy and social situation can be documented. Universities are characteristically lightly managed institutions and beneficial regional effects may simply flow out of the teaching and research priorities set for themselves by the academic staff. At the same time, regional agencies may have not clearly articulated regional needs to the universities, particularly to individual academics responsible for the delivery teaching and research programmes (as distinct from universities' senior management). There may therefore have been many missed opportunities for productive engagement. To reveal these opportunities, it will be necessary for universities to enter into a dialogue with various stakeholders in the regional development process. These stakeholders are likely to include:

— Central Government bodies responsible for funding higher education;

— Local and regional elected authorities;

— Employers and employers organisations (e.g. chambers of commerce);

— Arts organisations

— Regional media

— Lower tiers in the education system including schools and colleges

— Recent graduates, present and prospective students

In the context of national and international influences, each of these groups will have distinct goals and missions, means of delivering on these, financial drivers and constraints and customer/client relations. The nature of the interest of these groups in the well-being of the local community and how they can be articulated to universities will also vary. Unlike universities, which seldom have a defined territory, many of these bodies will be required by law to operate within a defined administrative area. The difference in the degree of permeability of territorial boundaries will create difficulties for dialogue that will have to be overcome.

Central to any dialogue between universities and regional agencies will be an appreciation of the latest thinking about the nature of the regional development process. A brief discussion of this area of academic enquiry now follows. The enormous transformations in the nature of the capitalist world economy since the mid-1970s, have had major implications for economic development strategies and their governance.

First, the stability of production systems, product markets and national corporate relations have been undermined by the rate of technological change, most notably through the widespread effects of generic or carrier technologies such as ICTs. Technological innovation and access to resources for innovation (skills, knowledge, information) have therefore become central to the competitive strategy of firms, which have developed new flexible structures to better utilise and capture such advantages on a global scale. States have recognised the need to maintain a position on the leading edge of technology if they are to maintain employment and growth, and hence there is an increasing attention to policies to support and promote R&D, innovation and technology transfer.

Notwithstanding this policy orientation, the globalisation of finance and of the organisation of production - underpinned by ICTs that permit the flexible reshaping and reconfiguring of investment and resources - has weakened the bargaining power of the nation state. International bodies have encouraged greater freedom in the flow of goods and information such that now it is the nature of the production locality as much as national market characteristics that determines investment decisions.

Not only has regional or local intervention become more important to economic success, but there has also been a qualitative shift in the form of local policy towards indigenous entrepreneurship and innovation, and to providing a more sophisticated environment for mobile capital so as to maximise local value added (R&D and other high status jobs, successful and therefore growing firms). The importance of this perspective for managing firms and localities has been neatly captured by Kanter in her recent book World Class which is significantly subtitled " thriving locally in the global economy". According to Kanter, future success will come to those companies, large and small, that can meet global standards and tap into global networks. And it will come to those cities and regions that do the best job of linking the businesses that operate within them to the global economy. She argues that forces of globalisation are so powerful that communities must connect the global and the local and create a civic culture to attract and retain or " embed " footloose investment. The challenge is to find ways in which the global economy can work locally by unlocking those resources which distinguish one place from another.

Kanter goes on to argue that in the face of these globalising pressures, organisations have no alternative but to continually improve and attempt to be world class by paying attention to what she calls the 3Cs—concepts, competence and connections. She links this to geography by suggesting that " world class places can help grow these assets by offering innovative capabilities, production capabilities, quality skill, learning, networking and collaboration. " The location of universities in regions is a powerful facilitator of these processes - concepts links to research; competence links to teaching and connections links to the transfer to and from a region of people and networks grown out of universities. In order to realise such policy shifts, local policy has needed to be innovative and entrepreneurial itself, typically through drawing on a wider network of resources, negotiating and building alliances between local and other tiers of government, universities, private sector interests and non-profit organisations.

Thus the successful entrepreneurial municipality shifts from being an arm of the national welfare state to a catalyst for local co-operation and policy innovation. Regional success has been characterised by a range of different models, but with a common agreement as to the factors underpinning success: agglomeration economies, economies of scope, trust, networks of small firms and supportive institutions. Central to successful innovation are the structures and modes of interaction between knowledge producers, disseminators and users. Since technologies embody both people and ideas as well as physical artefacts, transactions involving extensive interaction and iterative communication are widely believed to be necessary as a means of facilitating exploitation.

This 'organised' method of exchange can encompass both physical technology and/or employees - including producers, disseminators and users - moving between institutions while maintaining close linkages for instance, between universities and linked 'spin-off' companies. Within this overall policy environment geographical differences in the nature of cultures, institutions and legacies of past industrial practices will clearly influence the effectiveness of the dissemination of knowledge between and within institutions whether at national or regional scales.

Differences are particularly evident if interpreted as uneven capabilities in effectively organising, through informal or formal means, market transactions. For example, Lundvall illustrates the importance of a common culture and language shared by users and producers to facilitate the transmission and translation of highly encoded information such as R & D results. Differences in training cultures and attitudes towards technology are also crucial to the effectiveness of modes of communication and exchange.

Studies of economically successful regions suggest that their success depends on 'institutional thickness' or 'social capital'. Although difficult to define, this institutional thickness is more than simply a strong presence of institutional bodies and practices supporting enterprise. The institutions should have high levels of interaction, leading to structures of domination or coalition that can achieve collective representation of interests, and a mutual awareness of a common purpose:

a 'collectivisation and corporatisation of economic life'. An attempt to shape the governance structures in local economic development, in a way that increases the likelihood of a beneficial impact must therefore be cognisant of the culture, social structures and politics of the institutional networks linking policy actors and the firms they seek to influence.

In the context of the role of universities in economic development, the most helpful approach to operationalising these ideas can be found in the concept of the learning economy which emerges from studies of national systems of innovation. In his study of national systems of innovation,.Lundvall, B. A., stresses the importance of interactive learning as the basis for innovation and change in modern developed economies. He defines the learning economy in the following terms. It is an economy where the success of individuals, firms and regions, reflects the capability to learn (and forget old practices); where change is rapid and old skills get obsolete and new skills are in demand; where learning includes the building of competencies, not just increased access to information; where learning is going on in all parts of society, not just high-tech sectors; and where net job creation is in knowledge intensive sectors.

Within the learning economy different kinds of knowledge can be identified.

— know what, that is facts and information.

— know why, that is principles and laws necessary to reduce trial and error;

— know how, that is the skills and capability to do something, skills that are traditionally acquired within the workplace; and finally know who, that is information about who knows how to do what and the social capability to establish relationships to special groups in order to draw on their expertise.

Each of these different forms of learning uses different channels for information exchange. In the case of know what and why, formal learning in school and universities is the normal channel. Know how depends on practical experience through tacit learning (for example, through apprenticeships) but also increasingly through network relationships with industrial and commercial partners.

Finally, know who is learned from social interaction via professional associations, day to day dealings with customers, sub-contractors and a wide range of other actors and agencies. Focusing on network knowledge, this is a hybrid form of knowledge that is neither completely public or completely private. It depends on trust not the market and is characterised by such considerations as reliability, honesty, co-operation, a sense of duty to others.

Network knowledge refers not only to the skills of individuals but the transfer of knowledge from one group to another to form learning systems - the institutional infrastructure of public and private partnerships. Because network knowledge is highly dependant on interpersonal relations, it can most readily be developed within a particular region.

To be effective in this increasingly borderless global economy, regions must be defined by the same criteria and elements which comprise a knowledge-intensive firm: continuous improvement, new ideas, knowledge creation and organisational learning. Regions must adopt the principles of knowledge creation and continuous learning; they must in effect become knowledge-creating or learning regions.

Key to such a learning region is the human infrastructure and the institutional mechanisms that foster interactive learning, and a central part of this infrastructure, in terms of the reproduction and adaptation of human resources, are universities. In the case of human capital, universities in many countries have traditionally produced raw graduates for a national labour market dominated by large employers, with little concern for SMEs or graduate retention in local labour markets. This model has begun to break down in response to changing patterns of employer demands such as the decentralisation of large corporations into clusters of smaller business units and the greater role of smaller businesses as sub-contractors, suppliers, franchisees etc.

Such trends have important implications for the skills required of graduates and the location of the firms' recruitment decision. It is therefore not surprising that regional agencies are promoting graduate retention initiatives as a way of upgrading the stock of higher level local skills. In parallel with these demand side changes the expansion of higher education provision together with rising numbers experiencing the need to change career later on in life is leading to a growing supply of mature local students for undergraduate and postgraduate programmes.

Notwithstanding these developments, very little is known about the flow of students through higher education into local labour markets and how this relates to the overall economic performance of regions. Yet a key characteristic of the learning region is the way in which knowledge is transferred from one group to another to create learning systems. In terms of universities this includes knowledge of the appropriate skills and competencies required of the workforce.

What constitutes " appropriate skills " will depend on the overall regional development strategy, be it indigenous development based on local enterprise, exogenous development based on attracting inward investment, or a combination of the two, for example by upgrading local suppliers to support and " embed " inward investment. In this context, the analogy between regions and organisations is one where the shift from personnel management based around handling individual employment contracts and personal development to human resource management which harnesses people development to the strategic objectives of the organisation. So the key question becomes: " Does the region include a human resource development as part of its overall strategy? " This question raises a number of specific challenges concerning the type of training programmes, what institutions are best placed to provide the programme, and where within the region or for that matter outside should this provision occur.

So an obvious requirement of a regional human resource strategy is information about future labour market needs. Given the long time lag between the identification of needs and the development of the necessary skills, one of the fundamental requirements of a learning region is the sharing of intelligence between the education and training system and employers. In addition to ensuring that the education and training system produces people with the flexibility to respond to changing labour market circumstances attention has to be paid to the specific skills and competencies required by particular industries and/or occupations.

Labour market intelligence focuses on the direct contribution of universities to the economic success of their localities. A further question concerns the indirect contribution of universities to the social and cultural basis of effective democratic governance and, ultimately, economic success.

Regions or localities that are rich in such networks 'encourage social trust and co-operation because they reduce incentives to defect, reduce uncertainty, and provide models for future co-operation'. In so far as universities are by tradition classically " civic " institutions, they can play a key role in the development of the cultural and political determinants of socio-economic success. A key challenge is to enhance the role which universities, and their staff and students, play in the development of such networks of civic engagement, and hence in the wider political and cultural leadership of their localities.

Implications of many of these processes of globalisation and localisation that have been outlined have yet to be addressed by most universities. The scale of the challenge should not be underestimated. Adjusting the curriculum to rapidly changing needs of employers and the labour market provides a good example. In terms of Lundvall's description of the learning economy, whilst universities have been good at the know what and know why aspects of education, and are improving on the know how aspects through incorporation of the tacit learning acquired via work placements into teaching programmes, the know who dimension is altogether more problematic.

Progress on this front implies a deep relationship between research and teaching based on the sharing of the network knowledge of the research endeavour with students at all levels. When considering their relationship with industry in a regional context Universities need to consider themselves as being located at the head of a supply chain which is devoted to the provision of knowledge.

The distribution channels for this knowledge are through students (projects and placements), graduates and post-graduates, as well as through published and contract research and consultancy that leads to new and improved technologies and management processes. But unlike a business enterprise situated in a similar supply chain position, universities devote relatively little resources to marketing their products in the form of graduates or to responding to signals about what the market wants. They simply have a sales department, in the form of the Careers Service, which has no ability or mechanisms to match output (quality, quantity or specification) to customer needs.

The market place is, of course, extremely complex because it is composed of the totality of organisations that currently, or might in the future, employ graduates. At one end of the spectrum are tightly regulated vocational markets like medicine, architecture, law and engineering. At the other end of the spectrum are the largely unarticulated demands of SMEs. If universities are to play a more active role in economic development, it is vital that they understand the market, segment it and use this information to guide their teaching activities. This means not simply responding to currently expressed wants but actively researching the dynamics underlying changing employer needs and treating students as clients and employers as the end customer.

In some countries the fact that this approach is far from universal can be partly attributed to the student funding regime which currently rewards " production " but not " sale ". In consequence the marketing function is often poorly developed. If universities were in part rewarded for the delivery of graduates into employment, including local employment, they would clearly have an incentive to put more effort into marketing and economic development.

But becoming a market led organisation requires a major change in university culture. It implies a strong sense of institutional purpose whereas universities remain dominated by academics whose principle professional loyalty is to their national or international invisible college rather than their parent institution.

The "new production of knowledge" involves partnerships with the users and beneficiaries of research that transcends institutional boundaries and which are difficult to integrate with formal institutional planning and resource allocation. According to new patterns of strategic alliances between academic groups based on complimentary competencies may occur but not between institutions within a region.

Improved integration of universities with regional development will not be readily achieved by top down planning mechanisms at either the institutional or regional level but by ensuring that the various stakeholders in the regional development process - education and training providers, employers and employers organisations, trade unions, economic development and labour market agencies and individual teachers and learners - have an understanding of each others role and the factors encouraging or inhibiting greater regional engagement. For example understanding that universities and labour market agencies work in the context of national higher education policy and labour market training targets, employers of global competitive pressures to downsize, outsource etc. and students of personal financial constraints on investment in learning.

While national governments may seek to increase the engagement of universities with economic development, the means of achieving this goal is far from clear, particularly in the context of the value universities attach to individual autonomy. Such autonomy is associated with a diversity of institutions, often on a regional as well as a national scale, a pattern which has evolved historically. For those universities with a strong research base, regional issues may be of minor concern. Such institutions see themselves as serving the region by attracting students from outside with those students who remain adding to the local stock of human capital. They also contribute to attracting inward investment and possibly embedding that investment through training and research links. Such institutions thus contribute to exogenous regional development.

Nevertheless, even within research based universities, certain departments, degree programmes and research activities will have strong regional linkages. Alongside such institutions in most regions are those where serving the local and regional community remains a central component of their mission. Regional universities also have national and international links that can provide gateways for local firms and students to the wider world. Finally, between these extremes there may be universities which are trying to develop their research base in selected fields and in the process devoting considerable resources to " going global ".

Determining which particular mix of institutions and more importantly mix of teaching and research programmes would best underpin the economic development of a region is a key challenge. With the right form of incentives in terms of government procedures for university assessment and leadership development programmes, it might be possible to ensure that the appropriate signals reach and are embedded into the programmes of individual universities.

As regards assessment, regional criteria could be incorporated into national teaching and research assessment exercises. In addition, a strong case can be made for establishing a regional assessment process undertaken by universities themselves. Such assessments could be done with the aid of consultants with expertise in economic development and higher education management. The assessments would cover institutional organisation, teaching, research and other services actually or potentially relevant to regional needs. The outcome of the assessment could be linked to a government development fund for pump priming initiatives which seek to enhance the university's contribution to economic development. Institutions would be free to participate in such a scheme and/or confine it to those parts of their activity that they deem to be regionally relevant.

A number of questions will need to be addressed in such assessments. These include:

— *Synthesis*: Does the university recognise that by its very nature the territorial development process is broadly based embracing economic, technology, environmental, social, cultural and political agendas? The university is capable of contribution to this process across a broad front, not least by highlighting the interconnections across these various areas.

Indeed regional engagement provides an opportunity for reasserting the unity of the university as a place based institution.

— *Collaboration:* Are procedures in place to support inter-university collaboration? All universities in a region have an interest in raising participation in the lifelong learning process. " Growing the market " is to be preferred to mercantalism and this will involved collaboration within and between levels in the education system, including schools and colleges.

— *Partnerships*: Are the objectives of partnerships clear? Partnerships are for the long term and need to move beyond the identification of additional sources of funding to dialogue that affects the behaviour of participants.

— *Mapping and Measuring:* Who talks to who about what? The university's pattern of regional engagement will need to be mapped and the flow of information down these channels measured. Intelligence about the flow of students into academic programmes and subsequently into the regional labour market is a fundamental measurement task for the university.

— *Human Resource Development*: Is the regional agenda incorporated into institutional.HR policies? New agendas need new skills on the part of administrators and teachers and these need to be recognised in the university's HR programmes. Focus: What is the distinctive contribution of the university to the regional agenda? Notwithstanding the potential breadth of its contribution the university will need prioritise those areas where it can make the most cost effective contribution to the development of the region.

— *Geographical Identity:* What are the unique feature of the region to which the university can contribute? While there are global, economic, technological, social and cultural drivers of the development processes, these interact very differently with specific regional development trajectories. The university will need to develop a collectively understanding of its region in order to identify particular opportunities for engagement.

— *Regional Policy*: What are the main drivers of regional policy? Regional and national agencies have a suite of policies to address regional development. The university's need to understand these policies and identify areas where they can support and reinforce these policy objectives. Leadership: What role does the university play in regional leadership? In addition to responding to established policy, universities have the capacity to set regional and national agendas. This involves more than injecting good ides into the policy process; it also requires building the institutional capacity to take these ideas forward.

— *Teaching and Learning*: Has regional labour market intelligence influenced the shape of teaching and learning programmes? Whilst mechanisms are being put in place in some universities to respond to the regional research agenda, less progress appears to have been made on linking teaching and learning to regional needs.

— *Mainstream:* Has regional engagement become part of the academic mainstream of the university? Whilst many universities have established gatekeeper functions it remains unclear how far this has influenced mainstream teaching and research.

— *Communications:* Are regional needs and priorities communicated through universities? In addition to strategic engagement, there will be opportunities for regional engagement generated externally and internally that will need to be communicated around the institution. Newsletters, electronic mail and established fora provide an opportunity for such communication.

— *Research and Intelligence*: Is the university providing the region with intelligence for its forward planning? In order to shape the regional development agenda the university's will need to draw upon its global network and external information and tailor this to regional needs.

— *Responsiveness*: Is the university able to respond quickly to unanticipated regional needs? Economic development is opportunistic as well as strategic. If windows of opportunity are not seized regionally the advantages will be taken up elsewhere. The university will have to put mechanisms in place to respond, for example with new courses and research programmes

Alongside such assessments it would be necessary to have a programme of human resource development targeting those individuals inside and outside of universities that have boundary spanning functions relevant to joint working on economic development. One of the key factors of success in regional partnerships in the presence of " animateurs " who act as gatekeepers between different organisations/networks. A small number of staff in universities, labour market and economic development agencies and dynamic businesses hold positions in which extra-organisational networking is a central feature of their job. People who hold such position will do so by virtue of their personal and professional competency; they nevertheless require developmental support for their own professional improvement, and moral support from individuals and groups around them.

For the most part the necessary skills and attributes are intuitive and learned through practice; however the growing need for such people suggests that some more fundamental training and support is required. Relevant skills include: networking; facilitation; working with alternative cultures; setting up projects; planning and contract management; raising financial support; personal organisation; supervision and personal support techniques; insight into organisational policies and dynamics. The establishment of such a development programme for individuals engaged in the university/ regional interface would be a further small positive step towards its improved management. Similar strictures apply to other stakeholders concerned to raise regional competitiveness.

Universities in a Changing Environment

For the last two decades, the number of suppliers of higher education has increased, creating a marketing problem of product differentiation in which local uniqueness can be emphasised. More stop-at-home students and a rising demand for continuing professional development will be a feature of future development.

Many quangos are looking to universities for board members. Universities can satisfy a requirement for independent analysis, a neutral forum and local leadership, especially in economic development. Greater private sector engagement in the local community can stimulate new alliances with universities. Reorganisation and new priorities in the Health Service incorporating non-medical disciplines, present major opportunities.

Increasing scale, complexity, speed and scientific intensification of industrial R&D is undermining the linear model of innovation Changes in the organisation of industrial innovation include: decentralisation of R&D and integration with production; greater role for small firms and customer/supplier relations in innovation Government is pressuring for more demonstrable direct benefits of public investment in science. There is a widespread belief, based on a few examples, that technology transfer processes can be localised.

Geographical change is producing a shifting local environment for universities: suburbanisation of city centre activities; inner-city decay; shift to small towns; north-south shift. New industrial dynamics include manufacturing decline and service sector growth especially tourism and cultural "industries". The growth of the voluntary sector (care in the community) is replacing some state involvement in community services. Universities are part of shaping/ameliorating trends (eg., role in city centres; city marketing).

Ancient universities where the physical form and functioning of the city centre is dominated by the university: the image and perception of the place is synonymous with the university but where the institution itself is not locally orientated. Municipal colleges rooted in places which are not strongly identified with higher education. Metropolitan red brick/civic universities with strong regional identities. Post-war out-of-town campuses in large cities or in small towns where there has been limited local rooting. Decentralised multi-site campuses spread around a region.

Administrative areas are seldom appropriate for statistical purposes necessary to use the local labour market area in which the majority of employees live and work. There are wide variations in the degree of self containment in terms of purchasing of goods and services according to size of city and location of city vis-à-vis other centres. The larger the area of impact assessment the greater is the degree of self-containment in expenditure terms, but the smaller the relative impact.

Different services have different catchment areas depending on their specialisation and propensity of consumers to travel which in turn is related to frequency of use. Examples: sports facilities may be local, technology transfer regional and international. Administrative territories are important for funding purposes.

Institutional plans define specific local communities, some are laid down by statutes in the case of "old" universities. Multi-site "new" universities are staking out territory by the creation of new satellites (eg., Northumbria: Carlisle; Durham: University College, Teesside). Two-tier definitions are common (Sunderland: Wearside and the Northeast; Warwick: Coventry and the West Midlands). Greater regional emphasis is given in the institutional plans in the north compared with the south, and greater priority attached to community links.

Technology transfer is one of the main external linkage activities and generally the most important issue in mission statements in terms of local interaction. This reflects industrial demand, local development prospects (indigenous development cf. mobile branch factories), pressures from government. The transfer of products which embody technical knowledge is not the most important form of interaction. Much interaction is in non-commodified form through learning by doing and movement of individuals. The chain link model best describes a process in which the industrial innovation cycle is linked at all stages with the corpus of scientific knowledge . Firms and scientists must find appropriate partners worldwide; in contrast local small firms are much less likely to provide scientific challenges and pay for support.

Research grants and contracts involving industrial partners are important mechanisms. In aggregate Universities in more successful regions have higher income from these sources. Income from research councils and from industry follow a broadly similar pattern but with some exceptions.

There is a key role for management schools as decisions to invest in technology and its effective use depend on the awareness and competence of managers Some management schools focus on the special needs of small businesses, but this can undermine the achievement of research goals. Non-scientific knowledge (eg., politics of overseas countries, languages) has an important role in support of marketing by local firms.

University buildings generally add to rather than detract from the quality of the built environment. The central location of many universities and the access they provide to the public means that they play an important role in the sense and quality of "public space" within the city. Current expansion 'on the cheap' is undermining this quality. Changing university research and teaching needs has undermined the case for maintaining some of these spaces.

For more locally rooted universities the robustness of local demand may be central to survival. University planning needs to recognise the importance of local environmental resources in three spheres: business, local government and central government. For most of these groups, the university remains a "black box" within which organisational procedures seldom follow business and government practice. The challenge is to identify mechanisms for better structuring university/community relations whilst recognising these procedural differences. However, community links should not be regarded as a panacea for too many community ills.

Central activities (estates, personnel, purchasing, industrial liaison) operate separately with limited lateral communication in terms of community implications. Key interactions are decentralised through individuals and departments, with little central knowledge of what is going on. An audit of existing community linkages is required before any new structures are put in place. Universities should undertake a one-off questionnaire survey of all community-based activities with this information then being mobilised for the benefit of the whole institution. Each area of activity (eg., contributions to economic development, the built environment and social and community development) needs a clearly identified node or socket within the university into which individuals and organisations in the local community can plug. Representatives of nodes need to be brought together on a regular basis to drive through a community development strategy; this should be informed by analysis of the university's own capacity and of community needs.

The local authorities are the most appropriate body to draw together the various agencies representing community interest in the university and developing a shared strategy. Likely additional participants in the development of such a strategy include TECs, health authorities, chambers of commerce, enterprise agencies, the police service, integrated regional offices of central Government.

Universities and Economic Development

In UK National Higher Education Policy provides the context for university engagement with economic development. Whilst recognising the role of universities in " serving local and regional needs " this recognition has not been translated into funding formulae. Very little analysis of the available data has been undertaken to define those needs, for example in terms of geographical flow of students from home areas, through university courses into employment in different parts of the country. Published UCAS and HESA statistics suggest that between 18% and 48% of English undergraduate students attend a university in their own region, between 30% and 57% take up employment in the home region and 8% and 70% are employed in the region in which their university is located. Data for an individual university suggest important differences in the employment status and type of graduate finding employment within the immediate region. The absence of such regional analysis is not surprising given the priority attached to competitive funding, the lack of incentives for inter-institutional collaboration and for work with local industry in the research assessment exercise, and the disciplinary basis of teaching quality assessment.

The appropriate organisational framework for higher education provision at a regional level - competition for market share, formal collaboration, regulation of institutional roles or full integration into a federal structure - that can best serve the needs of different types of region is a key issue for further research. In the absence of a regional policy within higher education, other parts of government have either implicitly or explicitly provided incentives for universities to engage in economic development.

The drivers for adoption of a regional development role in relation to the curriculum include the desire of universities to improve the rate of entry of graduates into employment by tailoring courses to the needs of local companies, job placements, etc. Inhibiting factors in this cell include the lack of student demand for regionally relevant course (eg, engineering); student number caps locking universities into an historic pattern of provision; the absence of regional human resource strategies to guide course planning; lack of reward for academics for short courses or sub-degree level teaching; the role of national professional accreditation bodies; limited academic links with the regional training system below the senior management level.

The budgetary incentives for regional engagement in teaching arise from the growing number of " stay at home " students. The disincentive is that the new programmes that might be necessary to attract these students have to be introduced at the expense of established programmes because of aggregate student number caps. A key incentive in terms of serving students is the possibility of creating ladders of opportunity especially for mature students through access and franchise arrangements.

Support from TECs for local graduate retention and to integrate work based learning in the curriculum is a further positive factor. Set against this is the limited public support for part time students; patchy involvement by TECs; an over-emphasis on graduate placement compared with the development of higher level skills; a focus on provision of courses delivered at a certain place and time rather than flexible learning opportunities; the problem of matching graduate attributes to SME needs.

In terms of the research mission of universities, the emphasis in science policy on wealth creation through industrial links and the pressure from government offices for collaborative HEI actions has strengthened the case for regional activity in the minds of senior university management. However, the failure for this message to reach researchers in departments and the lack of individual incentives (eg, promotions, grant regimes) for regional engagement have generally outweighed these influences.

Universities devote relatively little resource to marketing their products in the form of graduates or to responding to signals about what the market wants, not least because the funding regime currently rewards " production " and not " sale ". Market segmentation regionally and by type of employer, taking account of the changing nature of work, is one way by which universities can grow their business. Universities need to understand the forces of globalisation that are impacting on employers internationally, nationally and regionally and which are feeding through into the demand for graduates by industry and occupation, in terms of the courses and skills required.

Key business responses to global pressures include outsourcing and concentration on core competencies; related supply chain management challenges; fragmentation of public services; search for productivity and service quality improvement through use of information systems; external penetration of local markets previously protected by distance (eg, direct tele-sales). These forces interact with specific conditions in different regions and need to be assessed by universities in developing their regional role.

Employers may also be segmented into three major types.

— Type A (the larger mature organisations) are the traditional graduate employers with well established recruitment procedures able to pick and choose universities and students according to their profile.

— Type B (the rapidly developing company) is emerging from downsizing, outsourcing, management buy-outs, privatisation etc of larger corporations or from fast growing independent starts. Such companies have a high demand for graduates but are much more difficult to reach by universities than Type A; they are the key to regional development strategies based around indigenous development.

— Type C (traditional small enterprises) include recent start-ups, mature owner managed family businesses without a history of graduate employment. These companies find selecting, screening and absorbing green graduates highly problematic. It is in this area that the gap between employer requirements and the output of traditional undergraduate degree programmes is greatest.

In terms of career trajectories, graduates may move not only between occupations and industries but between different types of organisation, either by choice or structural change. This has implications not only for initial training but the need for assistance with career transitions (after care services), a process which can most easily be managed at a regional scale. The need for responsiveness on the part of universities to changes in the market place in terms of type of employers, type of employment and industrial structures will require a strong regional dimension to university planning. Given that university based research on new technologies and new management procedures are important contributors to ongoing industrial and corporate dynamics, universities are well placed to use this internal knowledge to inform their own teaching programmes.

Differential regional demand has been superimposed on long established regional variations in the propensity of students to progress into higher education. Analysis by universities of the demand for their graduates therefore needs to be matched with analysis of the supply of traditional undergraduates, postgraduates and mature students by region.

Participation in higher education is most strongly influenced by parental and peer pressures (greater in regions with a higher proportion of graduates in the population at large); job prospects are another important factor (greater in economically strong regions). However, universities in less economically strong regions which can demonstrate good employment prospects by offering courses linked to local employer needs may be able to counteract this effect. In terms of students choice of institution geographical factors (town and distance from home) are almost as important as the course.

The economic and cultural vitality of the locality in the choice of institution by students is a major incentive for universities to engage in economic development. The lack of weight attached to career prospects reflects the limited career information fed into the student decision making process. This points to a stronger role for universities career services and alumni offices in marketing universities. For students wishing to remain in their home region or to have employment opportunities within the region of their university, mobilising links with local employers should be an important strategy.

For exapmle in UK 38% of all students in higher education are aged over 25 and the location of an institution is a major influence on their choice of programme. According to one survey, 43% of mature students study at an institution less than 40 miles from their home, compared with 19% of the under 25's. In this context the debate about lifelong learning has unfortunately not been closely linked to that on universities as regional institutions. The contribution of non-vocational courses to the development of local communities through raising cultural awareness and thereby combating social exclusion needs greater emphasis. Student financial hardship amongst both traditional and mature students is a major influence on attendance at the local institution. Not only are there regional variations in social structure but also in the opportunities for part-time work whilst studying. If the stock of human capital in less favoured regions of the UK is to be increased in order to raise industrial competitiveness many of the regionally specific socio-economic barriers to participation in higher education at various stages would have to be lowered.

The contribution of universities to regional development needs to move beyond simple economic impact statements to consider the way in which " top down " national policy for higher education can have differential regional effects. At the same time " bottom up " regional initiatives.are changing the characteristics of the higher education system at the margin. The concept of the " learning region " can provide a common ground between these top up down and bottom up perspectives.

Regional policy now recognises that one of the keys to raising regional competitiveness lies in enhancing the skills and competencies of the working population at all levels. Research on national systems of innovation suggest that it is not only the skills of individuals that matter but also the way in which knowledge is transferred between one group and another to create learning systems - the institutional infrastructure of networks within and between the public and private sector which supports economic development. Because of the importance of inter personal relations such networks have a strong geographical bias. So key a facet of a learning region are networks which effectively communicate to the education and training system the skills and competencies required of the workforce into the future.

In the North East of England, universities engage with these networks in six ways. First via a TEC/VC Forum, convened by the Government Office North East, and which has spawned various sub-groups of officers. Second, the universities own forum, Higher Education Support for Industry in the North (HESIN). Third, TEC financial support for numerous initiatives related to graduates and employment. Fourth, TEC/University strategies which identify key roles for the university as a major business, supporting existing businesses, supporting people and in exchanging experience in support of strategy development. Fifth, engagement with inward investors through tailored training programmes for new staff and joint research links. Six, ERDF funded technology support measures in universities linked to regional industrial development priorities. The North East exhibits a great deal of networking activity which increasingly involves universities. What is less clear is the precise role that the different networks play in the economic development process and the contribution expected of universities in each of them. The step from information exchange to action which influences in a significant way universities as partners in the economic development process and which would characterise the learning region has proved difficult.

To be effective in this increasingly borderless global economy, regions must be defined by the same criteria and elements which comprise a knowledge intensive firm; continuous improvement, new ideas, knowledge creation and organisational learning. Regions must adopt the principles of knowledge creation and continuous learning; they must in effect become knowledge-creating or learning regions ". For this learning to take place, the individual partners have to be open to external influence and this requires change within the higher education, industrial and regional economic development systems.

The higher education system has shown itself to be very responsive to the establishment of new assessment regimes in relation to the funding of teaching and research; criteria which have a strong regional dimension now need to be incorporated into these regimes. In teaching quality assessment, the attachment of a greater weight to employability skills within the curriculum would lead to greater regional engagement.

In research assessment, new incentives are required to encourage engagement with the tough challenge of knowledge transfer, including transfer via teaching undertaken in association with local companies and organisations. Such assessment regimes will need to be underpinned by more relevant data, particularly concerning the flow of students through universities and in terms of their subsequent career trajectories. If employability, including regional employment, were criteria of assessment the incentive to make better use of existing data and establish longitudinal records would be greatly enhanced. Many of these changes will require the acquisition of new skills on the part of academics and administrators at all levels within universities.

Universities will need to incorporate engagement within the regional development system as a key criteria in their human resource development strategies. In terms of the industrial system, one of the key characteristics of a declining region is a fragmented private sector, unable to aggregate its demands in a way that can be clearly communicated to the educational and training system.

There are various business leadership teams championing urban and regional regeneration in which individual members of universities play an active part, but the overall impact of such teams is limited because the various initiatives are not " mainstreamed " within either business or university.

Strategies for the Future

To prepare future generations for a sustainable future young people should be made aware of the complex nature and the interrelatedness of environmental issues as well as the multifaceted relations between environment and sustainable human development. They should learn to think not only in terms of threats and problems, but also of challenges and solutions instead and act accordingly. They should learn to understand that such solutions demand close cooperation between experts from a great variety of disciplines, cooperation and mutual understanding as well as of practitioners, theoreticians and policy-makers, and of people from all different sectors of society and walks of life. They should also learn how to do this in practice and, in this way, to understand what the expression "*think globally, act locally*" really means.

Universities, indeed all institutions of higher education, should first and foremost set a good example in their own housekeeping. They should confront their students with issues of sustainable human development, not only when they attend specialized major or minor programmes focussing on those issues, but also while dealing with topics in disciplinary programmes with clear consequences in the field of sustainable human development. Environment should be part and parcel of specialized university education. Here we should align the educational process with the policy process.

Universities should try to make, through their research, a major contribution to the understanding and solving of issues of sustainable human development, including ethical aspects. Universities should effectively interact with the society that supports them and share up-to-date and focussed knowledge with regard to sustainable development, without restrictions, with each other around the world and with all interested partners in society. Six key-actions are recommended:

— Create a university platform for a sustainable future to enhance synergy in knowledge, thought and actions of all organizations in higher education, including students and staff, prepared to work together on a more effective contribution of higher education to sustainable human development through teaching and research. Part and parcel of this effective contribution is an adequate preparation of graduates to function in the future world of work. Convene this platform every year in the framework of UNESCO's NGO-consultation. Make this an inclusive, not an exclusive platform, inviting representations of the business community, public authorities, NGOs, etc. The UNU could be an obvious choice to play a facilitating role in the development of this platform and its activities.

— Create an electronic network by establishing a major website including electronic discussion lists to facilitate the active exchange of ideas and information as well as to share examples of good practice in university housekeeping, management, education and training, research and knowledge transfer with regard to sustainable human development. This network should be linked to the International Registry of Innovative Practices that currently is being developed by UNESCO. Universities experienced in the use of ICT to create and support learning environments could be invited to play a leadership role in establishing and developing such a network, based more on substance than solely on the means of delivery. UNU-Press could produce essential information in the form of CD-ROMs for those partners in the network for whom electronic communication still involves too much time and/or too high costs.

— Establish a sustainable future award scheme for initiators of excellent, innovative contributions to sustainable human development in all three areas:

  — university management/housekeeping,

  — teaching and training/dissemination, as well as

  — research and development.

  Special attention should be given to the best case studies that integrate environmental concerns in disciplinary problems. Separate competitions could be arranged for each discipline. Short-listed entries could be published in electronic and printed form. In this way, one could build up good teaching resources.

— Develop a "preparing for a sustainable future audit system on a voluntary basis. The audit would focus on the structures, strategies and mechanisms in universities that contribute to their performance in this respect. The audit should focus on support to the participating institutions in order to improve incrementally their performance in contributing directly and indirectly to the improvement of the environment. Associations like the Commonwealth

Universities, the Talloires Group, CRE-Copernicus, the Association of African Universities (AAU), the Association of Universities in Asia and the Pacific (AUAP), and IAU could play a leading role here. Such audits should be based on self-assessments followed by assessments by peer groups. The audits should not be "stand alone" events, but part of a process which includes, among others, follow-up visits to support policies to improve the performance of individual universities.

— Start a feasibility study to identify in very practical terms the potential of universities in their different geographical, economic and socio-cultural settings to contribute on the university level and as major stakeholders to the further implementation of Agenda 21, to begin with the Local Agenda 21. This study should contain many good practice case studies that should help to illustrate possible ways and means for universities in the pursuance of the goals of sustainable development. One product of such a project could be a sort of "manual." The involvement of other stakeholders should be considered. This idea might fit into the proposed key-actions 2 and 4. Invite UNU and university associations active in this field to support such a study. The CRE-Copernicus Secretariat is prepared to play and active role in this key-action.

— Establish a special fund for direct mutual transfer of knowledge between teachers and researchers from developed and developing countries, among others, by organizing workshops as well as common projects in research, education and extension activities.

4

Challenges of Higher Education

In this world of massive, continuing and unpredictable social and technological changes, education has taken on a particular significance as a means both of understanding and of coping with such complexity. In spite of the frequency with which we are exhorted to adjust to change, it is difficult to realize the quite staggering impact of its increasing rate of acceleration. Higher education is one of the most durable forms of education. Universities have a long history and one in which their continued survival and, frequently their flourishing, is a remarkable story. It is doubtful if they have been through more difficult times over their many centuries than at present.

Quality Challenges in Higher Education System

Quality has become a major concern in higher education. This is because meeting society's needs and expectations towards higher education depends ultimately on the quality of its staff, programmes and students, as well as its infrastructure and academic environment. The search for 'quality' has many facets and the principal objective of quality enhancement measures in higher education should be institutional as well as system-wide improvement.

The quality of higher education is a multidimensional concept. As stressed by Donald Ekong, one approaches it through the composite concept of 'quality assurance', which implies that 'All the policies, systems and processes are directed to ensuring the maintenance and enhancement of the quality of educational provision within an institution. A quality assurance system is the means by which an institution confirms to itself and to others that the conditions are in place for students to achieve the standards that the institution has set'.

The concept of quality assurance implies that quality can be understood as adaptation to what is required by the institution, i.e. that the goals set have been reached in a manner consistent with fixed quality criteria. This definition is still very relative and leaves the door open to different interpretations as to the level required, owing to the diversity of tasks and goals and also to the influence of contextual factors on the choice and practicability of performance criteria. These considerations and the analyses made at the regional conferences lead to the conclusion that 'quality is inseparable from social relevance', that is, it is a quest for solutions to society's needs and problems, particularly those connected with the building of a culture of peace and sustainable development. They also lead to the conclusion that quality is not centred exclusively on products but also on the processes initiated by the system when it operates as a coherent whole in order to ensure this social relevance.

Challenges of Staff Development

The chief wealth of leading-edge enterprises lies in the quality of their human capital, this is all the more true for higher education establishments, so complex and demanding are the tasks (education, research and services) required of them. On the part of teachers and researchers they demand not only particularly great ability but also involvement and ethical values meeting the requirements of a quality directed at social relevance. A quality assurance policy therefore means identifying the required skill and attitude profiles before laying down a policy of teacher and researcher selection based essentially on merit, and applying it rigorously. But this also means managing careers so that progressively evolving needs match the available skill and attitude profiles, which calls for policies for the continuous training of teachers and researchers and the appropriate back-up strategies.

A quality assurance policy also implies working to motivate staff. This starts with a policy of conferring on teachers a suitable social and financial status comparable with their opposite numbers in industry. This furthermore implies policies to counter certain imbalances and develop 'well-articulated policies, remove gender inequity in education and, more importantly, promote the advancement of women in the entire society. This should include measures implemented by the institutions of higher education themselves. We suggest that meaningful affirmative action be taken in all possible directions. Women's associations and networks should be fully supported. A systematic and coherent policy of gender research and case studies should be implemented and their findings widely published...' (Dakar, para. 45).

As a result of the various developments in society and the higher education institutions, staff quality is going to depend increasingly on two types of major change. The first change concerns the training of teachers, who are increasingly having to adopt more innovative and interactive teaching ideas and methods, to use the resources offered by the new IT and to encourage their students to use them. 'Teachers and professors ... must be offered a training that enables them to integrate the use of ITs to their teaching programmes. This training will prepare them to act as multipliers of the use of these technologies'. The second change concerns the introduction of incentives and structures requiring researchers to work in multidisciplinary teams focusing on thematic projects and thus to abandon their habits of working exclusively in solitary isolation.

Insufficient attention, and insufficient resources for research is one of the worrying problems which higher education must tackle and whose nature varies with the region. In the developing countries, the burdens of teaching and supervision are sometimes such that high-quality research is impossible and researcher status is an empty word or is useful only for demanding additional funds. In certain very-low-income countries, the living conditions of teachers/researchers are such that moonlighting takes up the bulk of the time of those doing research.

In the more developed countries, the problems are different: some teachers divest themselves of their teaching duties because research is better for their career and because scientific criteria are the main factors in appointments and promotions. Others have chosen to invest first and foremost in teaching for reasons of personal preference or because of difficulties in doing research, depending on the case. If such an investment is not properly recognized by the establishment in its career management, the establishment will find that it is harbouring a great many frustrated individuals who may have a negative effect on a high-quality research policy.

Higher education institutions are generally labour intensive organisations. The quality of the staff these institutions are central to their effectiveness. In business and the professions there is a wide recognition that the skills of their staff need to be continually strengthened and enhanced. In the face of challenges from national and international competitors the better companies are investing more resources in the continual training and re-training of employees at all levels. They focus not only on the competence of their staff, but also give time to stressing the need for commitment to the organisation's goals and to promoting a capacity to change. They are crucial to national aspirations for economic development and, if such capacity building aims are to be achieved, the institutions will have to make the most effective use of all their human resources. In some academic fields it is said that the total of human knowledge is doubling every five or ten years. It is thus almost impossible for an individual staff member to remain in touch with the subject without a conscious investment in scholarship and self-tuition. When these knowledge advances are allied to similar changes in pedagogy, learning materials development and the use of technology, the scale of self improvement required becomes massive.

For administrative and support staff there are equally rapid changes in management processes, techniques and technology. In considering any strategy for developing human resources an institution must consider all its staff; administrative and support personnel can play crucial roles in helping students to learn, and in enabling and facilitating an environment that favours learning. If non-academic staff are committed to the goals of an institution, they can be valuable partners in working with academic colleagues.

The boundaries between categories of staff are blurring, as graduates assume jobs that would previously have been taken by non-graduates. In libraries, computer centres and laboratories those jobs once labelled "non-professional" are being filled by people who will expect to be challenged and to have careers which allow them to continue learning. To deny them staff development would miss a massive opportunity for the institution. In developing countries one of the biggest problems is that of obtaining and then retaining staff.

In no country are higher education institutions immune from severe pressures and challenges. Not only do governments talk to one another about funding, but the growing globalisation of higher education imposes similar burdens and threats on every institution. Among the principal challenges which affect human resource development are the following:

a) *the growth in demand for higher education* is a world wide phenomenon whether one approaches it from the standpoint of an age participation ratio of 35% or of 5%. UNESCO has charted the expansion in student enrolments from 13 million in 1960 to 65 million in 1991. In many countries the rate of expansion has exceeded that of the economy, while the reluctance of some countries to contemplate cost sharing has posed a major problem for their public sector financing. In institutional terms the expansion of numbers has placed pressures on facilities of all kinds.

b) *financial constraints in all countries* mean that governments can no longer fund higher education to the same extent as previously. Apart from asking students and their parents to share the cost, their response has been to call for continued efficiency savings (or simple cuts) in institutional budgets, which has led throughout the world to more severe staff student ratios and heavier workloads for academic staff. Another government response is to expect institutions to generate more of their income from non-governmental sources such as industry or commerce. This places new demands on academic staff who are expected to master entrepreneurial skills in converting their specialist knowledge into market-oriented services. One irony of the situation is that institutional budgets for human resource development are often the first to be cut, just when they are most needed, in times of severe financial difficulty. In many countries the reduction in funding for state institutions is leading to a growth in higher education provision by the private sector.

c) *a focus on basic education* has persuaded many developing countries to limit their support for higher education. Many bilateral donors have followed the messages from Jomtien and reduced their funding for higher education. Within many countries the reputation and public image of universities and the students in them has not helped their cause of getting more finance from either government or industry.

d) *the government and public expectations of universities and other tertiary institutions are* that they will be able to serve wider audiences of students, at different levels, in different ways. Thus among the new expectations will be: an ability to handle a growing proportion of part time students (usually meaning longer hours for staff); willingness to teach a greater number of mature students; the assumption that an institution can serve regional populations using links to associated colleges or providers; an ability to offer distance learning and face to face tuition in "dual mode", that is using the same materials and the same staff; an expectation that institutions can instil a set of "general transferable skills" in all their graduates so that employers needs are more fully met that faculty are all outward-looking and sensitive to the needs of their community; that staff have technical competencies which can offer research and consultancy services to industry and commerce in the area. These expectations place a great onus on institutions to give much more formal consideration to the needs of their stakeholders in their strategic planning and to involve their communities in advising on their institution's development.

e) *A concern for quality* of the product has accompanied the expansion in numbers and the reduction in funding. There is an inevitable fear that "more means worse" and quality will suffer as mass higher education becomes a reality. Governments, parents and students are asking questions about the teaching/learning process and are expecting institutions and funding bodies to monitor the quality of the processes and their outcomes. This questioning adds new pressures to academic staff, not only through the new accountability and reporting procedures, but also through having to be more explicit about the way they conduct themselves and more formal in the way they evaluate the effectiveness of their work. They must also be alert to the different ways in which they can maintain quality with larger class or group sizes.

f) *Technological change affects all disciplines and expects staff members* to be alert to the latest innovations in teaching method and research support. It is evident that there are at least three sets of distinguishing factors: the age factor in which younger staff members feel more at home with technology; the discipline factor in which some academic subjects are more affected than others and the developing country factor in which the gulf between "technology haves" and "technology have-nots" is widening. Even though access to the Internet will eventually enable developing country universities to remedy some of the deficiencies in their library and information services, this will only partly help to close the gap.

g) *The importance of increasing women's participation* among staff and students presents institutions with a clear challenge. As regards students this will affect their admissions strategies, their student support services and sometimes their teaching practices. Thus, several categories of staff may need to be involved in the solution. An even harder challenge faces those seeking to achieve a higher involvement of women in the higher ranks of teachers, researchers or institutional management. Whether the blockages to change in these two areas are in attitudes or processes, the problem requires a strategic review, followed by firm action, if it is to be resolved.

h) *The demands of the labour market* are changing dramatically and inevitably affect those institutions which seek to be responsive to national or regional demand. Some industries in developed countries operate in a global market place and thus recruit on an international basis and compare one country's graduates with another's. It may be unwise to ignore global or regional perspectives in the curricula in any courses which aim to serve these industries. Patterns of employment are also changing; courses which once met national needs are now irrelevant. New offerings are required in areas such as telecommunications, tourism, health care, financial services, food technology and transportation studies. Students who fear unemployment after graduation will now be seeking the more vocational and relevant courses which enhance their chances of employment. In many countries they will also need to be taught how to create their own employment opportunities, when traditional employment is not available. All these changes require increasing adaptability among academic staff, particularly those in declining disciplines.

i) *Effective management demands new skills* within institutions which may not always be present among those who traditionally lead at either central or faculty level. There are widespread complaints within institutions about "new managerial cultures" driving out the old academic collegial spirit, yet the very complexity of the demands on senior institutional managers makes it essential for them to be fully professional. In seeking to achieve this they must learn to adapt commercial management techniques sensitively to the academic environment and never forget the mission of the institution they serve. The technical skills needed by today's institutional managers call into question some of the traditional management structures and job specifications. If it is thought that the answer rests in greater devolution to Deans and other middle level managers, this means that a large number of people in each institution will require management development support.

j) *Roles of people in higher educational institutions*: These daunting challenges are likely to have a considerable impact on the work and role of each of the main participants in institutions. All will be affected by a number of common changes and trends. There are seven:

— a need to be responsive and able to change (in line with the changing policies of governments, external demands and social pressures);

— a call for greater awareness of international perspectives in the content of courses;

— the demand for relevance in the curriculum from employers, governments and students;

— the need for more inter-institutional co-operation, in some cases with the burgeoning private sector;

— awareness of the institution's role in society and the need for it to contribute to national development or the local community;

— a growing emphasis on quality teaching as opposed to research as a worthwhile career goal for academic staff ;

— the increase in demand for postgraduate provision, particularly in those countries with relatively high participation rates in HE.

These have varying impacts on each category of person in an institution and we now review this in turn For institutional leaders, Rectors, Vice Presidents, Pro Vice

Chancellors etc, the challenges are immense. They bear the brunt of decision making and strategic direction in new, very uncertain environments.

Leadership skills will be essential as will communications and persuasive skills in convincing academic colleagues of the need for changes to long established habits. The leadership role will centre on the management of change and on reconciling the essential need to adapt what are usually conservative institutions with the opposition and unease that such change will cause. Thus, the key roles for such leaders will include:

- — providing strategic guidance and a vision of where the institution should be going;
- — persuading external bodies such as business, donors and alumni to contribute funds to replace those which government has withdrawn;
- — encouraging innovation and an entrepreneurial culture and ensuring that institutional processes support rather than hinder this;
- — maintaining commitment to institutional goals in a community which is instinctively suspicious of such things.

Institutional managers such as deans and heads of departments are the Executive Head's partners in ensuring that change happens. They have a leadership role at the discipline level and a key part in implementing institutional change. They will share in the turmoils of managing institutions in transition: however, because their responsibilities are at a more detailed level they will need to have more tangible competencies. Among them will be the following:

— people management skills, such as team building and helping staff to develop themselves academically and professionally;

— numeracy and understanding of financial and cost issues;

— IT awareness;

— sensitivity to new developments in the external environment, such as competitive threats;

— customer consciousness;

— strategic awareness of the institution's position;

— understanding of how to use institutional decision making processes in a collegial environment.

Academic staff in their teaching role face probably the biggest set of challenges to their working patterns. They bear the ultimate burden of having to "do more with less", as student numbers increase without matching funding. They are being asked to teach a wider range of students (mature, disadvantaged, part time etc) in different ways involving new methods and technologies. Their accountabilities are being sharpened and made explicit, as quality reviews and assessments examine what they do. In this harsh environment a model teaching staff member would have the following competencies:

— awareness and understanding of the different ways in which students learn;

— knowledge, skills and attitudes relating to assessment and evaluation of students, in order to help students learn;

— commitment to scholarship in the discipline, maintaining professional standards and knowledge of current developments;

— awareness of IT applications to the discipline, both as regards access to materials and resources world-wide and as regards teaching technology;

— sensitivity to external "market" signals as regards the needs of those likely to employ graduates of the discipline;

— mastery of new developments in teaching and learning, including an awareness of the requirements of "dual mode" tuition with face to face and distance learning using similar materials;

— customer awareness, as regards the views and aspirations of stakeholders, including students; understanding of the impact that international and multi-cultural factors would have on the curricula;

— ability to teach a diverse range of students, from different age groups, socio-economic backgrounds, races etc, throughout a longer day;

— skills in handling larger numbers of students in formal lectures, seminars or workshops than hitherto, without the loss of quality;

— development of personal and professional "coping strategies".

This list of required competencies is unlikely to come together in any one person, so that there will be a tendency to encouraging staff to specialise in some of the skills and functions described.

Academic staff in their research role are also under pressure. Universities are increasingly basing their assessment of research quality on the ability of researchers to raise outside funding, as well as on the volume of research conducted and published. Funding is much more competitive than before and often open to international bidders. Research customers are becoming more demanding in the quality of the proposals they require and the final end products they expect. Among the skills which researchers now need are: proposal writing; networking and fund raising for projects; managing PhD students and researchers; project management, particularly relating to international partnership projects.

For academic support staff in libraries, resource and computer centres there are matching demands. The new technologies require mastery of new techniques and software in searching for information and a changed role in supporting users of these support services. The boundaries are blurring between the roles of teachers and those advising students on information retrieval. Both are helping the student to access knowledge held elsewhere and both are faced with calls for help over longer hours from a wider ability range of students. The UK's Dearing Report endorsed this finding "where communications and information technology has changed the nature of learning and teaching, there is a need to review and redefine the roles of academic and support staff within institutions".

For administrative staff there are also new competencies required: information technology skills are now taken for granted similar financial pressures mean that cost awareness and sensitivity to the need for value for money in all administrative processes have to be in the bloodstream customer sensitivity is a key skill, now that budgets are so often devolved to Deans or Schools and central administrators find that they have many academic clients to serve flexible working practices become essential as management costs are being continually trimmed.

Some of these are echoed for technical and manual staff who find themselves under equal pressures to be more cost effective, flexible in work practices, more technically alert and more sensitive to what their customers want. In addition, they are often now expected to work in a less secure environment due to threats of outsourcing or contracting out their services. As a reward for accepting this uncertainty they are sometimes being brought more into decision making and being asked to share in the corporate ethos of the institution.

In developing countries there are particular problems which affect the ability of staff at all levels to acquire the skills described. When even professorial staff are paid salaries so low that they are not enough to feed their families, it is not surprising that staff should spend much of their time on second and even third jobs. Retaining good staff in such circumstances is often only possible because the institution provides a house at a negligible rent, but finding funds and time for staff development is much harder. In addition, the pressures of survival limit the time that even the most professional staff members can devote to activities other than the basic teaching load. In small states there are unique staff development problems arising from the small size of higher education institutions. Limited human resource capacity in the country makes senior staff very dependent on external partnerships for advice and information. Multi-skilling within institutions is unavoidable and there are inevitable shortages of specialist staff.

Training Needs

A response to the challenge is integrated and holistic. There are two other key principles which should be borne in mind: staff at all levels should be encouraged to expect to embark on lifelong learning, in their discipline and in the skills needed for their workplace and their role in their institution; any staff development programme must adopt multiple mechanisms for its delivery offering flexibility of access. In this model world institutions would have clear strategies covering staff development for all levels of staff at all stages of their career. These would be integrated with their human resource strategies so that selection and promotion criteria, career planning and staff appraisal processes were all influenced by the strategy.

Initial training for academic staff in institutions is not universal and after a generation of worthy campaigning by staff developers it is still unusual to find countries where it is even mandatory to have completed any training before being confirmed in an academic post. However, even here the pedagogical pressures have rarely provided what might be called a systematic, professional approach to personal development. There are exceptions to the dismal picture. India has 48 academic staff colleges, funded by the University Grants Committee, which offer initial training and limited mid career training to all university staff.

In the United Kingdom the recommendation in the Dearing Report to create an Institute of Learning and Teaching in Higher Education for all academic staff is being energetically pursued. Formal training for higher education staff was required in the former Soviet Union and Eastern Europe. In West European states such as

Great Britain, the Netherlands and Germany institutions have been making efforts to strengthen pedagogical training and the status of staff development programmes has increased. Some of the hopeful signs are: Laws passed in several German Laender to the effect that applicants for a professorship have to give evidence of their pedagogical skills; inclusion in staff contracts, in some institutions in Germany, Norway and Great Britain, of clauses binding new academic staff to attend staff development courses; The creation in France of a national plan for practice-oriented pedagogical training down to postgraduate applicants for teaching posts; The growing number of staff development units within universities; even though the norm is for non-mandatory courses, the numbers participating on them are increasing.

Continuing professional development (CPD) in the academic teaching profession has had as disappointing a history as initial training. Even though some regard it "an essential rather than a desirable objective, an obligation rather than an option - both a professional expectation and duty and a responsibility that institutions have for their staff", this view is rarely echoed by those allocating resources within institutions or at national level. Voluntary courses offered by an underfunded central support service are the normal approach to meeting this need.

The basis on which staff are employed is changing golbally.Several countries are abandoning universal tenure for academic staff in favour of term contracts and the jobs of many non-academic staff are subject to the threat of competitive tendering from external contractors. Many institutional managers find that employing part time contract staff is a cost-effective way of meeting their need for teaching skills. For teachers and researchers in particular one should ask, what is the continuing place of tenure and other forms of job security within the institution? Will increasing insecurity affect the willingness of the individual to adapt and change in line with the institution's requests?

Salaries and salary structures have in the past been based on civil service precedents. Yet now there is competition from private sector institutions of higher education with deeper pockets and differing reward systems. How realistic is it to consider relating pay to performance and what effect will this have on the demand for staff development? Can the state sector compete by stressing non-pay benefits such as the status of a professorial title? Will institutions be able to retain good people in this way? Is there not a case for devising incentive systems, as institutions' earnings from the commercial sector increase? If staff bring in extra income from non governmental sources, what share of it should they be able to retain?

If policies are generous to the individual in this respect, will it prove divisive within the institution if it favours staff in disciplines with high potential for such earning? The implications of the changes in the age profile and study mode of students are that working hours for all teaching staff in institutions will lengthen to stretch into evenings and weekends. This can be resourced by expecting existing staff to work in a different way or by using job-sharing, part time helpers or non-academic support staff. The culture within which academic staff operate has always favoured research excellence at the expense of teaching.

There is a large gap between the massive need for staff development and the present small level of activity, and this should lead some governments and institutions to plan an increase in their provision. In many cases they have much to learn about how to plan, develop, promote and then deliver staff development programmes. Inter-university Co-operation can play a major role in helping those at the beginning of the learning curve benefit from the greater experience of others. Such co-operation can be provided through national networks or professional associations of staff developers within a country or within a region; however, few countries have such organisations and therefore most institutions will need to seek an international network.

In recent years UNESCO's Networks for Staff Development have met this need, as they have brought together groups of those concerned with staff development in higher education institutions. Such networks have cost implications in the first instance, although their existence can bring operational economies by helping members to share resources and learn from each others' experience. Areas where such network co-operation can prove valuable are:

— advice on the staffing and structure of staff development units within institutions; support in developing and drafting strategies for staff development;

— advice on the training that staff developers need and the personal skills and competencies they should have;

— exchanges of course content on all aspects of improving the quality of teaching (but care must be taken to amend the content for cultural differences);

— joint development of staff development programmes;

— information on good practice in operating and managing a staff development unit;

— direct exchanges of staff between members ;

— supplying names of good training providers and feedback on their performance,

— advice on how to collaborate with other providers in the private and public sectors.

Once networks of this kind are created, they allow a variety of interactions between members: exchanges of materials, easy communications with each other, the opportunity to meet at network workshops, staff exchanges between members, jointly run activities, formal problem solving consultancy visits by one member to another etc. The great value of networks is that they provide an easy forum for peer review and debate; if this can include people from other cultures and environments, there will be the added bonus of the diversity from a range of international perspectives.

There have not matched the need and that much more has to be done if the human resource capacity of our higher education institutions is to be fully and effectively utilised. We now consider some suggestions for action by the various participants. The organisation able to adopt these proposals will vary according to where authority lies in each country.

For all the staff in institutions the issue is one of awareness of the need for continuing development. What is often lacking is the strong push by them for the development of training and development opportunities. In the absence of this demand training providers sometimes find that the courses they offer are undersubscribed.

For institutional managers there are several areas where action is needed: every institution should prepare a staff development plan as part of its human resource strategy. This should state clearly what policies are as regards the level of staff development and training which each staff member is entitled to. It should define the roles that categories of staff are expected to fulfil and the staff development needs of those roles ; institutions should review their institutional policies relating to selection and promotion criteria, confirmation of contracts after probation and award of tenure and consider whether they should be linked to the achievement of any staff development targets; consideration should be given to making participation in staff development a mandatory requirement before promotion or entry to certain posts.

This should apply to both academic and administrative staff; the head of the institution should give firm backing and support to staff development as an institutional priority and should ensure that it receives adequate funding; each institution should establish a central staff development unit to develop and monitor institutional staff development policies, provide a programme of short courses and workshops and report to the Governing Body on overall performance of the institution in this area; the institution should seek to create a culture where participation in staff development activities is a regular feature of life and is welcomed; responsibility for promoting staff development should be clearly defined; one model is for Heads of Departments to be given managerial responsibility for helping members of their staff develop their performance and effectiveness, using central institutional or external providers as necessary; institutions should consider setting targets for individuals to join in CPD for particular categories of staff and should consider making some training mandatory (eg: safety, customer service) for some jobs.

For governments and national funding agencies there are several ways they can achieve effective staff development strategies. If they are in a position to control such matters centrally, they should modify the national systems of recruitment and promotion in order to stress the importance of staff development by making it mandatory at certain stages. If institutions are responsible for such matters, governments can make it clear that staff development has their strong backing by asking to see human resource strategies as part of their reviews of institutional strategic planning. They could even consider penalising those institutions which have not given proper consideration to staff development activities in their planning and funding. They can also directly fund innovations in staff development.

Governments can also promote collaboration and co-operation in staff development by providing pump priming support for institutional units or for a national association/network of professionals involved. Another approach is to establish a staff development unit at national level, preferably with the backing of the national organisation of vice chancellors/rectors, to support universities' units and act as a forum for the discussion of staff development policies and mechanisms for collaboration. Ensuring that institutions have an adequate advisory and support service is a proper national function.

For international agencies and donors there are various options for support. The idea of continuing international Staff Development Networks has already been mentioned, but this assumes that countries and institutions are already committed to the idea of staff development. There may be an opinion-forming and educational function before this, in which agencies such as UNESCO or IIEP could run workshops for national policy makers in higher education on the issue of encouraging institutional staff development. Other possible interventions would be: sponsoring surveys of good practice and disseminating them through networks; organising an informal "network of networks" in staff development;

Promoting joint projects between new staff development units and experienced ones in different countries; helping staff in developing countries maintain their professional competence by funding participation at conferences and sabbaticals; funding a UNESCO chair in staff development in higher education; running workshops on specialist topics using international experts; providing consultancy advice to national staff development agencies in response to demand; sponsoring surveys of good practice outside higher education identifying ideas which might be imported; promoting the development of performance indicators or management statistics allowing institutions to compare their staff development activities with each other.

Challenges of Curriculum Development

An increasing number of factors have an impact on the need to modify curricula and can therefore affect their quality: the knowledge explosion and the burgeoning of new disciplines; the increasing need to adopt a multi- and trans-disciplinary approach in order to understand natural and societal phenomena; diversification and regionalization of education courses; the proliferation of short courses and the need to provide crossovers between the various short and long courses; the desire for greater social relevance in a changing world. These pressures compel higher education to adopt three major types of qualitative change in their curricula: changes in goals, in methods and in the structure of curricula as they relate to one another.

Basic training must not be viewed simply as the accumulation of knowledge but must be directed at acquiring skills, the chief ones for each student being: their ability to mobilize their knowledge and related skills in order to analyse complex situations, resolve the problems they pose, be capable of teamwork, be capable of providing logical justification for their choices and show foresight. Value education will develop the capability and habit of reacting as a bona fide committed intellectual and as a responsible and co-operative citizen in order to build sustainable development and a culture of peace. To ensure that such basic education and training are of high quality, it is important for them to be rooted in real-life settings and not to be just a formal exercise that has no meaning and is non-transferable. The place where training takes place and its immediate environment are the initial means of exercising the aforementioned skills and attitudes and thus of responding to the explicit or implicit demands of the environment.

The networking of physical or virtual exchanges provides more extensive possibilities, making it possible to attain universality through comparison with other contexts and thereby also to reach a better understanding of the specific features of local contexts. Students thus learn, together with the partner institutions, to pinpoint common goals and specific goals more accurately and to distinguish more clearly between what is transferable as such and what must be adapted.

While the quality of curricula is contingent on the quality of goals, it is also highly dependent on the quality of teaching methods. As a result of mass education - without any proportional increase in resources - and the use of new technology, higher education faces the temptation to make greater use of transmissive teaching in large groups, which it is difficult to reconcile with the goals set out above. To meet the increasingly crucial challenge 'to respond to the mass phenomenon and not diminish, and even increase quality', this means a big effort of imagination by higher education. Methods which involve students more deeply in the management of their learning and the use of certain facilities offered by IT, whether in real time or at a distance, are routes which should be explored and cross-fertilized through exchanges of experience.

With increasing openness to training throughout life and in different places, curricula will have to adapt teaching methods to the characteristics of the population concerned: an adult with professional experience does not react in the same way as a young person just out of adolescence; an adult sent by his or her firm to acquire skills relating to a change of job does not have the motivation or needs of an unemployed adult who comes to study of his or her own volition in the hope of acquiring qualifications that will be useful. The increasing openness towards greater flexibility and lifelong learning schemes is leading, and will increasingly lead, higher education institutions to carry out a fundamental re-consideration of their curriculum structures so as to create a linkage, or an 'interstructuring', of curricula.

Against the background of a growing internationalization of curricula, higher education is being compelled to re-think the ways in which it organizes its curricula; it no longer does this in isolation but in conjunction with other institutions, and taking into account the increasing readiness to accept lifelong training. It is therefore necessary to continue the effort begun by the student and teacher exchange networks to define more explicit conditions for entering and leaving curricula and programmes that are open to exchanges.

Quality of Students

Access to higher education must therefore be governed by the merit principle, i.e. by the right skills profile. 'Determined efforts are necessary to increase access to higher education, especially for currently poorly represented groups. Distance education and open learning can play a major role in widening access'. Efforts are likewise needed to increase access to higher education 'for all groups in society'. Higher education must therefore increase the number of initiatives in order to 'guarantee the principle of universal access' and governments must establish positive-discrimination policies for those with fewer opportunities or in order to redress certain balances.

The Latin American and Caribbean Regional Conference even goes as far as to call for 'free higher education in order to improve equity and ensure an adequate quality and effectiveness of studies'. This demand, which is based on a literal interpretation of a clause in the International Covenant on Economic, Social and Cultural Rights (Article 13, para 2c), has financial implications and raises particularly acute problems in regions of the world where the states' public debt is particularly large.

Access to higher education by all students who merit it implies consultation with the secondary education sector and with the bodies involved in the transition from secondary education to higher education. Such consultation must take place in a spirit of mutual co-operation so that the 'educational chain' is strong and leads to high-quality secondary and higher education. An 'observatory' storing information on the follow-up of secondary students as they pursue their university careers would be particularly useful for providing the two types of establishment with useful pointers on how to improve the quality of education, ensure an improved policy of access according to merit, and look out for imbalances between sub-populations with different characteristics so that access is made more equitable. Higher education must collaborate on improving secondary education, ensuring that pupils leaving school at that level have mastered the necessary life skills, including those needed to pursue higher studies.

Student quality viewed in a spirit of greater equity implies that educational establishments must not confuse 'elite' and 'merit'. The concept of elite indicates a quest for the particular, while the concept of merit indicates a quest for the universal. Student quality also implies that students must not be left to their own devices during their studies but must be active participants in the life and management of the institution in order to develop an enterprising spirit, a feeling of responsibility and a culture of solidarity. It is important, furthermore, for institutions to set up structures that will provide social, psychological and educational guidance and assistance, so that students with problems can feel that there is solidarity and a determination to ensure that all those who deserve it reach the end of their training.

Infrastructure Development

Quality of education and research assumes the existence of an adequate physical infrastructure that matches needs. It also assumes, however, that such infrastructure is maintained and managed in the best possible way in the institution's interests, and not mainly for the convenience of the managers. These conditions are far from being met in too many higher education institutions. In some institutions in developing countries, the libraries are now no more than book deposits dating back more than ten years; laboratories are rooms with out-of-date equipment which is particularly useless because the basic items for experiments are lacking; lecture halls are designed for half or one third of the numbers using them; paper is a rare commodity which it requires long, costly and often fruitless efforts to obtain.

Quality of infrastructure will depend in the future on the attention paid by higher education establishments to the development of the new IT, distance learning and the virtual university. The initial outlay for their use is substantial. The investment needed to keep up with their headlong development is by no means negligible. The funding of research in this field calls for large sums and thus for access to the foundations, which are increasingly tending to redirect their investment to a few recognized centres of excellence, especially in the industrialized countries.

All these considerations explain the disarray among those who see the gap between rich and poor regions widening. While they recognize the importance of IT in improving the quality and relevance of higher education, they find it difficult to see how, without massive aid in conjunction with genuine co-operation between the state and external funding sources, establishments will be able to resolve problems as ordinary as: 'the scarcity and high cost of equipment, software and information in comparison with the North; lack of accessible telecommunications infrastructure; the telecommunications monopoly joined to over-regulation and high cost; instability of the electricity supply in many countries; lack of networks and interregional co-operation'. However, if it is borne in mind that IT is already producing radical changes in learning methods, priority will clearly have to be given to this topic.

The new technology opens up extraordinary prospects for learning and for the diversification of institutions, but the latter must bear in mind that, while it alters relations between teachers and students, it does not eliminate the need for direct contact between student and teacher and among students themselves, who depend on this interaction for their social development.. Besides the quantity and quality of infrastructure, attention must be drawn to the quality of the living environment in the higher education institution and to the quality of the external environment.

While the educational institution is a place of training which must stimulate students to take responsibility for their training, it is also a place of education: the living environment must bear tangible witness to the concern for what is beautiful (architectural design, room for the cultural dimension), true (unhindered access by students to data bases, places for debate) and just (participation in social projects, solidarity movements). But the university cannot be an inward-looking island; interactions between the internal and external environment must be creative, such as the reciprocal relations between campus and town, the pooling of certain resources, exchanges of data bases, and telecommunication networks. Such partnerships must be aimed at creating a mutual quest for quality in the interests of improved development.

Assessment and Regulation

Quality and quality-assurance concepts increasingly go together with concepts of assessment and assessment culture, as mentioned by all the regional conferences. By analogy with the concept of quality control dear to businesses in recent decades, the concept of assessment has been too narrowly equated with monitoring the relationship between actual and required performance.

Nowadays, however, assessment is interpreted more broadly to denote a process of gathering and processing of relevant, sound and reliable data so as to enable the parties concerned to take the necessary decisions in order to improve actions and results. Assessment as a form of control is an excessively static and restrictive process which is perceived as penalizing; assessment as a decision-making aid is more dynamic and transparent and is seen as having a training function.

Control is too often seen as a judgement on individuals; assessment, on the other hand, relates to collective actions and results which must be constantly improved and made more relevant. Thus, if we wish to meet the challenges to higher education throughout the world, a culture of evaluation must be established and reinforced in all institutions. This therefore means that goals must be clearly explained by and with the parties concerned in liaison with higher authority in order to make sure that the specific goals are consistent as a whole. This also implies that these goals are expressed as relevant and observable indicators for the efficient collection of data. This culture of assessment and self-assessment must be introduced and strengthened at all levels, from the students to the highest authorities, including teachers (these are still more accustomed in too many institutions to assess rather than to self-assess or be assessed) and researchers (where genuine research exists, there exists also a culture of assessment also exists which is carried out by the scientific community). But the institution must also introduce a culture of assessment both overall and with reference to the external, social and professional environment, in order to answer the following crucial question: does the institution contribute through its educational, research and service activities to the sustainable human development of the environment in which it is situated?

An assessment culture entails the setting up of banks of sometimes recurring data in order to analyse how the effects of actions change over time; other data are of a one-off nature, being targeted at specific actions which have a location in time and space but form part of an overall project. The gathering, management and analysis of these data bases consume energy, money and time. It is therefore important to ensure 'a balance between the costs and the level of quality improvement achieved.

A culture of assessment means a culture of regulation, i.e. a shared and interdependent study on the basis of a compendium of relevant information, of the strategies needed to improve the effectiveness of the operations launched or, if necessary, to readjust the goals and actions. A regulation culture essentially involves a culture of participation by those concerned by a project. Participation begins with participation by the students. It answers a dual purpose: firstly training, since it is impossible to imbue them with an enterprising culture without involving them in their training project, and secondly, opening-up to the outside world. The passion, generosity and even idealism of youth are essential forces which complement those of adults, who can help them with their experience and know-how in introducing key ideas and putting them into practical effect. Ideas govern the world, but know-how is needed to translate them into action and results.

A regulation culture entails the creation of communication facilities in the institution, with the participation of all concerned. All too often, malfunctions occur in the system for want of communication. All too often, the steps taken to deal with them prove ineffective because there was no real prior consultation. Yet it is not sufficient to create communication structures. Such structures are too often misused: participants arrive misinformed or inadequately informed; the structures become talking shops designed to consolidate or demonstrate power; decisions are taken in haste after long and frequently sterile discussions. A culture of regulation implies professionalism: properly prepared and managed communication arrangements; an ability to delegate to competent individuals so that they can prepare reliable dossiers; building on past experience; determination to assess the results of the decisions taken.

Challenges of Higher Education Researches

Higher education is now regarded as an institution not only for developing knowledge and training young minds, but for disseminating and applying such knowledge as well. The 20th century will be remembered for its intellectual discoveries of relativity and quantum mechanics, and for the interpretation of the structure of DNA—discoveries that have enabled researchers to unravel some of nature's secrets and the fundamental behaviour of some of its life forms.

The university's utilitarian perception of its mission, now regarded with greater emphasis and urgency, has come about largely as a result of these breakthroughs of knowledge in the natural sciences. Among the consequences of these discoveries could be listed the fantastic development of information technology and high-tech industries, the increase in life-expectancy (chiefly because of advances in medical research and nutritional science), and increased food security (derived from genetic engineering research). In all these, the university has provided much of the leadership; with the partnership of government and its agents, industry and international agencies either as research collaborators or as funding bodies.

It is such achievements, such triumphs of science, higher educational institutions should pursue knowledge only for its own sake. Of course there will continue to be programmes of liberal education devoted entirely to scholarly study of the major works of other scholars to help clarify and possibly modify one's previously held convictions. Pure scholarship will remain with us because of the persistence of the cherished value of freedom of thought and enquiry, that intellectual value upon which the life of the university as a place of research and teaching depends.

But in recent times, the immense contributions that university research has made to the national economy ironically places in jeopardy the future funding of such work. The university itself appears to be moving away from its ancient tradition of pursuing pure inquiry for its own sake precisely because of the pressures felt from underfunding.

The current triumphs of research are due in large measure to the provision of adequate financial support from government, from the private sector (through its industries) and from international agencies. The successes of the newly emerging economies in South east Asia—the present economic crises notwithstanding—provide sufficient evidence that in a science and technology-driven economy, it is the university that must be the powerhouse of the "knowledge economy." Now governments everywhere are expecting the university to fulfill its role as a major agent of economic growth.

However, there is a price to pay for this. The injection of public funds into the university for research requires accountability that may be directed by an outside body and not by reliance upon the university's own evaluative procedures. This may impact negatively on a tenet the university holds so dear: respect for academic freedom and autonomy of choice in conducting one's own research. In the same way, industry in the private sector is accountable to its shareholders who are typically more interested in their profits than in the pursuit of knowledge for its own sake.

Shareholders are likely to favour programmes and projects that yield immediately applicable results. The effect is that basic research will be the loser. Going after government and industry-supported research could lead to long-term consequences that are not easy to predict. The challenge now is to work out ways of catering for the interests of both parties in the research partnership. There is also the problem of research conducted outside the university. The total government expenditure for research is often shared between the university and other specialised national research institutes or centres, while multinational industries have their own laboratories for research. The conduct of advanced research is no longer solely the preserve of the university.

Research results obtained in national research institutes as well as in industry may be classified and so may remain unknown to the research public, sometimes until two or more decades have passed. No longer is all knowledge readily disseminated to all those capable of benefiting from it. The freedom to pursue research and to publish one's results, the freedom to communicate among researchers and to disseminate such research information—these cherished rights—are thereby compromised with predictably morbid consequences for the educational training of the next generation of researchers.

Inadequate funding, leading to the need to generate additional income from other sources, is one reason for the university and its researchers to move toward applied research at the expense of basic research. The need for funding has yielded the marginalisation of research motivated by a sense of curiosity generating from the intuition and the sheer intellectual power of individual minds. Yet fostering such work remains one of the basic missions of any higher educational institution, perhaps all the more so during times of socio-economic crisis.

Prior to the demise of one of the superpowers, national agencies used to support basic research principally for its potential applications in the military and in commerce. But now they have less reason to invest in it. Yet everyone recognizes the economic and social benefits of basic research: it produces background knowledge, it develops research skills, new techniques, instruments and methods that in turn yield economic benefits over a much broader range of production sectors.Also there is a symbiotic relation between basic research and technology, with each moving ahead increasingly faster because of the impact that one has upon the other. Thus inadequate funding for basic research has an immediate deteriorating effect not only on higher educational institutions themselves but on national economies.

Curricula of some of the most advanced universities encourage too early a specialisation for the student. A science student specialises in the study of nature but not of man; student of the humanities concentrates upon man, to the complete neglect of nature. The result is the existence of what of the two cultures. Some policy makers are students of the humanities with little or no interest in how the technological gadgets that they regularly use came about. Similarly, some scientists are hardly conversant with the appreciation of poetry or art or music. The public will better appreciate the work of the researcher if he has been prepared with an understanding of that public in all its dimensions.

Indeed our educational system should be guided by the scientific worldview that has emerged in this century, that is, the Copenhagen interpretation of quantum mechanics that states that there exist several mutually exclusive but complementary approaches to reality, since nature and society are too subtle to be described from any single viewpoint. The education of the scientist should include training in the social sciences, and that of the social scientist should include training in the natural sciences, so that it is possible for them both to apply their fullest potentials to national life and development.

Development is closely linked to environmental change. Two major causative factors have been identified as responsible for the degradation of the environment, with serious implications for the future of planet Earth. These are the increased consumption patterns and life-styles of the affluent industrialised countries, and high population growth rates in the developing countries. Sustaining these life-styles and catering for the minimum needs of the global community have led to a considerable pressure on our natural resources.

So, in order not to compromise the needs of future generations, the challenge to the researcher whether at a higher educational institution or in industry is to either identify alternative sources of energy which are renewable and are environmentally-friendly or, if we are to live with non-renewable sources, to find ways of decreasing the carbon dioxide emitted by fossil fuels.

How to achieve population stabilization has to be considered not only from a purely economic point of view but from human and cultural aspects as well. Happiness in some cultures means having many children while in others it is having one or none at all. All researchers, social and natural, basic and applied, have a role to play in our attempt to encourage a globally applicable plan for sustainable development.

Research on the management of the environment, is global and interdisciplinary. Fortunately, meaningful cooperation and collaboration is now possible because of information technology. We need to take advantage of this very useful technology. No doubt, the 21st century will raise even more problems but in the midst of difficulties lie challenges and opportunities. In all our deliberation, we need to ask ourselves what sort of human society we want to build in the next century; it must surely be one dominated by science and technology, but which engages the participation of all researchers.

To fulfil universities's role as a major agent of economic growth, governments should continue to fund basic research to levels. Governments of developing countries must create the necessary social environment that nurtures scholarship; they should also provide a reasonable percentage of their GNP to promote quality higher education and capacity-building in research, International organisations and researchers in the developed countries must help break the isolation often experienced by researchers working in developing countries, through such methods as creation of centres of excellence twinning and sandwich post-graduate programmes, Higher educational institutions and research institutes outside the higher educational set-up need to collaborate to promote the principle of universality of knowledge.

Higher educational institutions should ensure that the education of the researcher includes training in both the natural and social sciences, nature and society being too subtle to be described from one single viewpoint only, International organisations including International Council for Science (ICSU) and the International Social Science Council (ISSC), must prepare guidelines for their members concerning the ethics and responsibility in the conduct of their research.

Information technology has proven to be a powerful aid to the researcher; but its potential has yet to be fully exploited. Its recent forays into the higher education industry, through the establishment of the 'Virtual University', has led some to forecast the demise of the traditional university structure as it is presently constituted. This is because of the several advantages the 'virtual university' has over the traditional one: it encourages collaboration between universities and staff in distant locations; it affords the ready availability of first class libraries to students in varied institutions; and it is an excellent tool for cutting down costs.

The Internet is encouraging is the possibility of providing at lower cost the capacity to unite spatially disparate people. In this way, it enlarges the research community to include those outside one's physical neighbourhood, so that people with shared interests can interact while working in different places on the globe.

Currently, questions are being raised concerning the desirability and even the purpose of some of the research carried out in higher educational institutions. For although these institutions provide the technical tools of civilisation, they do not at present provide any guidance for their use. They are neither interested in ultimate ends nor can they predict ultimate consequences.

Typically, researchers are now faced with questions concerning the consequences of their work: what will be the consequences of biochemical weapons research for future generations, or of nuclear waste disposal, or of human cloning and other genetic experiments? How can our planet be saved from the current as well as for the future generations? Here we are dealing not just with technological and ecological questions but with moral dilemmas as well. The university cannot remain wholly indifferent to all values other than its cherished prizes of the search for truth and for funds, important though these quests may be. The "good members of society", duly trained by the university, should "go into life conscious of the deeper issues at stake and of the values involved in them."

Truth and its applications must be pursued with responsibility, and it is for this reason that ICSU has created a Committee on Responsibility and Ethics in Science, charged with the duty of helping to find solutions to problems concerning ethics and responsibility in the conduct of science. ICSU aims to ensure that the contributions science makes to humanity will be for our common well-being and for humane social progress. For, without such ethical vigilance, the distrust that some of the public currently has about science will most likely intensify at great cost to the progress of science. It is the challenge of the researcher to ensure that the two values of freedom and responsibility in the conduct of research are kept in their proper perspective, if the researcher is not to encourage the rejection of progress or modernity as an item of reactionary dogma.

The economic progress that industrialised nations have enjoyed was hastened because of the existence of the relevant indigenous capability in a social environment that nurtured scholarship. The gap between the developed and the developing worlds, which is widening at an increasing pace, will be narrowed only if the necessary infrastructure and local supports for high education and research exist within the developing world.

While most governments of the developing countries are facing serious economic crises, in the long run it will be to their advantage if a reasonable percentage of their GNP provides the resources necessary for the promotion of quality higher education and capacity-building in research. The advanced countries can also contribute in the effort to create an indigenous base for research by helping to equip researchers of the developing world for full participation in knowledge-based socio-economic development. Working as a researcher in a less than sound environment, with few exceptions, means working in complete isolation.

Autonomy and Academic Freedom

Over the past quarter century, the forces of modernisation have drawn heavily upon higher education. They have also contributed in no small way to profound and often radical transformations in that community itself. The drive to mass higher education in the advanced economies and the very substantial growth in the numbers of institutions and of students in the less advanced economies of the world, both testify to this process. Nor is this dynamic likely to be any the less vigorous over the coming decade and beyond.

The emergence of what has often been called "the Learning Society" amongst advanced technology economies, effectively the establishment of life long learning with its concomitant of knowledge updating and renewal for individuals, promises to be no less challenging in creating new expectations and demands amongst those who are likely to need - and make use of - such services and provision.

Growth of demand for higher education over the past quarter century and the distinct likelihood of its continuation well beyond the foreseeable future have, however, to be placed against a number of limitations, not least in the public sector, that of finance. Resource constraint limits the ability of higher education to meet current expectations with the quality often held to be necessary. Thus, in many countries, the credibility and standing of universities are increasingly subject to question.

One of the most pressing challenges facing universities today is that of resources - how to increase them; to diversify their provenance, to improve both their internal allocation and management and finally, how to meet the responsibilities society places upon universities whilst maintaining the recognised tradition of autonomy and disinterested service. Nevertheless, the accelerating pace of change contains enormous potential for development just as it presents formidable challenges.

It requires universities to embark upon considerable investment in adaptation, innovation, in developing sensitive and sophisticated systems and methods of management, in the definition and execution of the various alternatives which lie before them. It remains a fact however, that individual universities are far from being equal in the resources they command, in the ability of the student body they can attract or the esteem they enjoy in their communities. And whilst the speeding up of change and the demand by society that it be speedily accommodated are the watchwords of the hour, it does not follow that individual universities uniformly possess the same capacity to meet these exhortations.

Another factor which is in process of reshaping the landscape of higher education across the world, is the globalisation of economic and financial exchange and the international nature of technology. One may confidently predict that this factor will continue to operate and with increasing weight in the affairs and priorities of higher learning. For all systems of higher education, globalisation opens up the prospect of a higher level of interdependence across national frontiers than has been usual in the recent past. There are many reasons why this should be so and equally there are many which call for universities to make the effort to be part of this new dimension.

Increasingly, the conduct of research in domains directly linked to technology, biotechnology and medicine is characterised by sustained international cooperation. And judging the quality of research projects has long been subject to international peer review. The growth of the international dimension has been especially noteworthy at higher levels of training, particularly at graduate level.

Universities that lack entrepreneurial impulse and most especially in the area of economics and technology development, are not destined to flourish. The globalisation of the economy and the international flow of technology are not the only driving forces which bear down on the development of higher education. Equally potent are cultural, social and political differences which identify nations, peoples and communities and thus universities themselves.

The coexistence of finance, economy and technology which drive towards integration alongside the enduring presence of cultural differences, political and historic specificities and variety in systems of belief which seek to uphold their particular nature, makes for powerful tensions, and most certainly so when upholding such particular features often tends to involve denying the freedom of others to exercise similar rights or by threatening them with subjugation.

Universities lie athwart these two worlds. They are subject to the tensions which each separately generates. They are also subject to the tensions that arise when the international appears to be in conflict with other, more rooted, notions of identity and belief. If the path to innovation and a healthy dynamism lies in an arena, increasingly international, in which disciplines and institutions compete for repute, recognition and excellence, it has also to be recognised that the university is founded within particular cultures and embedded in a specific society.

The university serves as handmaiden to the burgeoning internationalisation of scholarly communication, of knowledge in general and of knowledge that applies to commerce between the Nations. But it is also the child of the cultures in which it is set. Its responsibilities also lie in protecting and advancing local cultural, intellectual and scholarly traditions. Viewed from a world perspective, the major and constant challenge which the university faces from now on, is to uphold a judicious balance between the pressure for change which comes from the process of technical development qua globalisation and the tensions created within civic society as a result of the impact of economic and technological change upon the social fabric. It is a delicate task and one ever renewed. It stands as an additional responsibility incumbent upon the university precisely because the university is both the agent and the recipient of economic and technological change.

But, such a task is no less delicate for the fact that it comes over and above such well-recognised obligations as acting as a vehicle of understanding between different cultures and communities and for rectifying, where possible, the social imbalances which result from poverty, exclusion and conflict. So that the University may fully assume the responsibilities which Society lays upon it, the University as an institution of scholarship and its academic staff individually need to be granted certain conditions of work held to be necessary for such responsibilities to be optimally fulfilled. These terms are contained in the two concepts of University Autonomy and Academic Freedom. The former relates to institutional self government. The latter relates to the individual members of academic staff. And, in respect of the freedom to choose what they will study, extends also to students. These conditions vary in their operational detail, in the degree to which they are applied in different countries and within countries, to different types of institution within the national system of higher education.

The generic feature which distinguishes the University from training, from compulsory schooling and post compulsory institutes of education is the freedom to learn for students and the freedom to teach for academic staff. By extension, the freedom to teach is held to encompass the obligation upon academic staff to contribute through enquiry and research to the advance of fundamental knowledge which shapes the particular area of study to which they are individually committed.

Academic freedom can be viewed as a functional condition which allows the University to fulfil its responsibilities to society; as a philosophic proposition and as a moral imperative. Not all those engaged in the academic community enjoy the same degree of academic freedom. Nor does it follow necessarily that academic freedom can - or should - be extended beyond academia. There is a view which argues it should be confined to those places and circumstances where it may be practised. This distinction is an exclusive one. It denies the notion that academic freedom leads on to the general right of Freedom of expression and to the general 'right to know'. Thus, the usual view of academic freedom is that, by definition, it applies to the academic community.

Such a view does not go unchallenged by those who view academic freedom as a sub-set of a broader and universal Human Right - that of the freedom of information and expression. This interpretation starts from the premise that academic freedom is a necessary condition for Human Progress. It links academic freedom to the broader issues of social advance in general thereby tying in academic freedom as an element in ensuring one dimension in Human Rights.

Knowledge, so this line of argument runs, is not finite. On the contrary, progress is shaped by the ability to question, criticise and to enquire. Ensuring progress is one of the responsibilities of academia. It is not, however, exclusive. Since the accumulation of knowledge through enquiry is a condition of Human progress and advance, academic freedom is a condition of that progress. It has, however, to be recognised that in practice, there are areas of research and enquiry to which this general principle is not extended. Research connected to national defence and sometimes to industrial R&D are cases in point. Thus, the issue of academic freedom should be debated within terms broader than the usual perspective of higher education.

In effect, the core freedom which lies beneath academic freedom is the freedom of enquiry and this, also by definition is universal. The latter definition will be discussed as a forward looking perspective to an issue which, in general, has tended to be debated in terms of historical antecedent. Other arguments justify the exercise of university autonomy less on the grounds of its being an historic *'droit acquis'* than on grounds of efficacity and utilitarianism. They draw upon contemporary developments beyond academia and in particular those found in other organisations, one of which is the modern enterprise.

It may be argued that university autonomy - that is the capacity of self-government - is no less a prior condition for universities to determine in what way they may and will respond to competition, whether for students, for resources or for repute. To be in a position to do so, however, it is incumbent on the university to develop techniques of management, administration and self -verification which balance university autonomy with the obligation to be accountable to society, to demonstrate efficiency in fulfilling its mission and transparency in its manner of achieving it. We have therefore to be aware of the elements of change which a closer association with the productive process implies for a less narrowly defined concept of university autonomy than the historic and perhaps traditional interpretation of the university's governing principle.

Academic freedom and university autonomy naturally imply the obligations to excellence, to innovation and to the advancement of knowledge, the former by individual academics and the latter by the institution

Academic Freedom and University Autonomy have tended to be regarded as a protection vis a vis arbitrary interference and are underwritten by formal legislative enactment or by the State's recognising the customary practices of the academic community. Though the responsibility of the State is not less central today, current developments whether expressed in terms of economic or administrative rationality - de-regulation', 'privatisation', 'decentralisation of decision-making" to the individual university or the greater importance attached to regional authorities - imply a more complex relationship with civil society. Today, Academic Freedom and University Autonomy are increasingly tempered by notions of Accountability and 'responsiveness to external interests'.

Academic Freedom and University Autonomy - has two elements: first, that for the foreseeable future it is highly unlikely that universities will return to a period of stability. Rather they will continually be faced with an evolving series of demands from different sectors of society and from the economy the more higher education becomes a central element in the latter. The second and in consequence, that for universities simply to "meet" whatever demands society places upon them is neither acceptable nor likely to be judged appropriate. The assumption is then that universities ought to be "pro active" or, put in other terms, that they are prepared to take the risk of seeing ways of anticipating and taking the initiative in meeting society's demands.

Today Universities stand on the threshold of society's realising that idea to which higher education has long subscribed - that is, the global transmission of knowledge. Globalsiation poses many issues, not least of which is he ending of that historic monopoly over the transmission and production of higher education universities enjoyed almost since their foundation. But the type of knowledge transmitted, the way it is transmitted and to whom, are not neutral processes. They carry with them values and priorities and thus assumptions about who is to receive what type of knowledge and for what purpose. Even assuming that globalisation does not lessen cultural diversity or undermine both specific knowledge traditions and the communities which have developed them, questions that have been basic within the confines of the Nation-State are becoming yet more pressing when placed in a global setting.

As public bodies or as private corporations, universities have long been involved in rendering accounts either to government or to Boards of Trustees representing either the public or the 'owners'. Thus, the right to institutional self government engages the responsibility of university to demonstrate full and formal compliance with the appropriate conditions, laws and procedures. The demand for greater transparency and the press for universities to show their achievements with greater precision have brought the issue of accountability and quality assessment to the centre of higher education policy. Though the tying of institutional budgets to quality targets is far from being universal, it is clear that the extent a university may effectively exercise self government is increasingly dependent on demonstrated efficiency and effectiveness.

University autonomy shapes the relationship between government, society and the university. It upholds freedom from arbitrary intervention. Yet the more higher education is driven by a market economy, the greater the number and variety of external interests with which the university will have to deal, seek support and, ultimately, rely upon.

The intensification of exchange ange between university and society is a direct consequences of policies of "de-regulation". But it also implies a new commitment, some would say a new moral responsibility towards ccivil society which extends well beyond the issue of financial support. And the greater the weight placed upon the university's commitment to "community service". New partnerships at local and sub-national regional level certainly follow from the need to diversity support and funding. But the 'return' of the university to civil society poses a number of questions about an enhanced and more active role it may play not only in the usual area of 'services to the community' and in greater attentiveness to "stakeholders". Such activities are also an act of social solidarity and responsibility by assisting that community to draw up the main priorities for its own development.

Freedom to carry out research and the obligation to publish lie at the heart of academic freedom. They constitute at all levels - individual, departmental and institutional - the bedrock on which public recognition of excellence and scholarly achievement, rests. As universities seek to increase external revenue sources, to develop closer links between industry and the university research base and to demonstrate entrepreneurship through setting up science parks, spin-off firms and business ventures, contractual agreements can limit this commitment.

The autonomy of higher education institutions must be strengthened and be accompanied by a high level of responsibility and accountability with the broadest possible participation of students, teachers and administrators in decision-making processes. Knowledge is a social asset that can only be generated, transmitted, criticized and recreated for the benefit of society, in plural and free institutions that have a full autonomy and academic freedom. However, the latter must also have a clear awareness of their responsibility and a will of service that cannot be turned down. Hence they will be prepared to search for solutions to the demands, needs and lacks of society. This is indeed a society it should be accountable to – as a requirement – in order to exercise fully its autonomy. This will require a culture based on autonomy for higher education institutions as well as of their constituent units it will also require solidarity and responsibility towards the institution as a project for promoting local development. Thus the need for accountability, which is indissociable from the concept of quality.

The culture of autonomy, responsibility and accountability implies from the outset that teachers/

researchers should have improved 'living and working conditions and emoluments of academics. Although this problem is particularly crucial in many developing countries, it nonetheless raises its head also in the highly developed countries where, in high-value-added sectors, one sees a draining away of the talent needed by the university whenever there is an excessively marked imbalance between salaries in higher education and those in business.Forging a close link between a culture of accountability (and therefore of assessment and regulation) and a culture of responsible autonomy (linked to the concept of merit) is one of the major challenges to higher education institutions in the next century.

5

Management of Higher Education

A higher-education institution may be regarded as a global system composed internally of interacting subsystems and involving complex interactions with the outside world. A higher-education institution interacts, in the first place, in various ways with the meso-environment, which imposes on it certain requirements and provides it with certain resources. But it also exists in a macro-environment which acts as a vehicle for certain geopolitical phenomena that exert pressure on it. While these environments exert various pressures, in its turn the higher-education institution influences these different environments, especially through what is called the 'educational income'.

A university education institution is composed of a set of sub-systems: for example, the university as a global system consists structurally of sub-systems in the form of faculties and departments. Over and beyond the structural level, however, it is also worth considering the level of the functions characterising both this global system and its structural sub-systems. The university education institution is composed crosswise of five interacting systems/functions and sequentially of two systems/functions relating to the flows that cross itFrom the sequential viewpoint, two systems govern the transformation process, namely the admission system for students, who form the higher-education institute's 'raw material', and the validation system, which specifies the characteristics which this raw material must possess when it leaves the institution.

The global system exists and evolves according to five fundamental systems: tasks, structures, resources , culture and management. This last system determines whether the seven systems composing the global system interact smoothly. Contrary to the narrow and outdated view sometimes taken of it, the management system does not consist solely in administering the institution's finances and material resources.

The management of higher institutions cannot be reduced to financial management based on purely economic criteria. One should take into account some criterion of equity and the criterion of social relevance applied to teaching, research and consultancy activities'. This extract sums up fairly accurately the concerns of all the regional conferences regarding ways of managing higher education and its funding.

The management of higher-education institutions is subject to ever-increasing pressure from a socio-economic environment in the throes of change.At Palermo the European Agenda for Change in Higher Education in the 21st Century stressed a number of points: the impact of European integration; the increasing demands made on higher education for quality services; an increasing trend towards the globalization and harmonization of teaching, learning and research; the substantial contribution of higher-education institutions to building the greater Europe of the future.

The Tokyo Regional Conference emphasized sharing of the expertise and experience of higher-education institutions and called for closer links between training, research, trade, transport improvement and rapid communication. It also asked for the pursuit of regional social goals to be encouraged and for national cultural heritages - the basis of identity - to be safeguarded.

The Dakar Regional Conference perceived globalization as a transcendent economic force based on distant power sources. Seeing the widening gap between developing regions and the others, it considered globalization to be much more of a threat than an opportunity: brain drain towards the highly developed countries; baneful effects of structural-adjustment policies on the social, cultural and educational sectors; increasingly severe public debt; flight by high-value-added industries to other regions; increased poverty, unemployment, hunger, disease and illiteracy; conflicts of all kinds; degradation of the environment. Yet, despite these dramatic findings, it clearly recognized that protectionism is no solution; a different vision, not governed primarily by anonymous economic imperatives, must be brought into play with the aid of states and higher-education institutions in a spirit of mutually dependent internationalization.

The Latin American and Caribbean Conference stressed the disparities not only between but also within regions, using a revealing expression: 'islands of modernity in an ocean of poverty'. At that conference, Juan Carlos Hidalgo drew attention to two major types of approach by the university at the dawn of the 21st century, which he called the 'university-company' and 'university-society' approaches. The main features of these approaches are summarized in the table 1

Table 1: Comparison of two approaches to the management of higher education

Key Concepts	1st approach: University-company	2nd approach University-society
Quality Evaluation	Quality is determined by the capacity of the graduate to integrate himself into the labour market. Market ideology is taken to the field of university education	Quality has a broader meaning. It is based on the notion of social profitability.
Autonomy	The university loses its autonomous nature as its activity is determined by market-induced demand. It therefore loses its capacity to decide what to research or teach.	Autonomous thought, i.e. the quest for truth and scientific rigour, lies at the heart of this approach. It therefore does not allow itself to be subordinated by the state or by particular links with ideologies or parties.
Access	Access is determined by the balance between the demand for professionals and admission and departure flows from the university. Admission restrictions can therefore be expected; the right to education becomes a privilege.	Education is regarded as a basic right of every citizen. The university's function is to train resources to meet economic, social, political and cultural needs. Quantity and quality must be reconciled, on the basis of the merit principle.

Research	Research is secondary. It is justified only when it helps to give a more or less immediate response to the demand for and needs of technology. Research and development expenditure must be left as far as possible to more developed countries.	Basic research and applied research and, more generally, technological knowhow are fundamental for two main reasons: they permit sust-ainable and autnomous development.
Education as a priority.	This is a question of priority. Where resources are lacking, higher education occupies a lower priority than other levels of education.	Education is a cumulative social process, an 'educational chain'. The opportunity cost of education is not an internal issue but rather an issue linked to other sectors of societal development.
Education as a cost and investment	Education is a cost to be minimized and must be dependent on the balance of public finances.	Education is an investment which permits greater economic productivity and improved cultural and social well-being.
Efficiency	The purpose of efficiency is to rationalize and minimize costs on the basis of cost-benefit analyses and econo-mic calculations.	Concept of effi-ciency cannot be restricted to economic and accounting criteria but must include joint quality-relevance equity criteria.
Training as a taxable base.	Through training the student receives a 'personal educational income' which will be profitable later. This income must therefore be taxable.	Educational income is not individual but an income generated outside the educational system. Training is therefore not taxable, on pain of encouraging igno-rance.

Nature of the state contribution	The financing system based on a state contribution is regressive and can even be described as reactionary, as the poor pay for the rich. Tuition fees would therefore be a less inequitable mechanism.	A financing system with reduced state intervention and the use of tuition fees is much more reactionary and regressive. Reducing inequities is a matter primarily of state policy regarding taxation and the apportionment of public expenditure.
Social equity	The system is more equitable if students finance their training themselves. It is therefore a domestic matter for the better off to fund the training of poorer students.	Making the system more equitable implies a deliberate and more comprehensive policy involving responsibility for government policies.

These ideas may seem rigid and it is true that elements of both systems are found in many institutions. However, in certain universities which are considered to be particularly successful, there are fairly strong pressures in favour of the first approach, even if this exists side by side with forces favouring a more traditional approach centred on the disinterested pursuit of knowledge paying no attention to pressures from the external environment. The conclusions of the various regional conferences reject the first approach but they also agree that the universal university cannot accept out-of-date 'ivory tower' attitudes and must move towards a more societal approach which combines concern for autonomy and independence of thought and the quest for truth and scientific rigour with an effort to respond to the economic, cultural and social needs of the environment and hence determination to play its part in sustainable human development.

The first approach ('university-company') is an essentially short-term approach: training must provide rapid responses to duly observed needs and guarantee a return. Basic research, whose results are difficult to pin down in the short term but essential in order not to suffocate applied research and the development of new technology, must be restricted to a few centres of excellence in countries which can afford to fund it. Under this approach, such centres are not necessarily situated in higher-education establishments; some of them are already integrated into major multinational companies and this will happen even more frequently in the future.

Wealthy countries and multinationals supported by all-powerful financial holding companies are thus increasingly taking over the development of knowledge as a source of wealth and power but not necessarily as a source of sustainable human development. When this approach is adopted we can therefore also expect research in the human sciences and the arts to be neglected since their economic and financial value is practically nil. We can also expect, the various types of disparities and inequities to become more pronounced. This management model for higher-education institutions, which emphasizes the short term and leaves the long term in the hands of interests which are too exclusively financial, is accordingly not recommended by the regional conferences.

The management model for higher-education institutions must take account of their function as observers and consciousness-raisers. Institutions must place their intellectual resources and independence of thought at the service of harmonious and sustainable human development. Their observer function consists in drawing attention in their own particular environment and in the external environment to situations – with their different economic, cultural, social, political, scientific, technological and ethical components – in which the True and the Just are being flouted. Their consciousness-raising function consists in anticipating the consequences of such situations, predicting the main trends affecting the future of society and imagining which scenarios are most likely to help to improve development.

Higher education must strengthen its capacity to perform a critical analysis, to anticipate and to have a prospective vision. It must do so in order to prepare alternate development proposals and face the emerging problems of a reality undergoing a process of continuous and rapid transformation, in a long term horizon. What is increasingly needed by higher-education institutions is therefore a model for forward management:

— there is a need for forward management of tasks in the face of an ever more rapidly changing world;

— for forward management of training structures in order to meet the compelling requirements of life-long education and the necessity for a more regional and international vision;

— for forward management of research structures in the light of the necessity for more interdisciplinary research in networked teams;

— for forward management of entry and departure flows with an eye to more relevant and higher-quality training;

— for forward management of financial, material and human resources in order better to carry out tasks and respond to trends;

— for forward management of sub-cultures inside and outside the institution so as to create an innovation-oriented culture serving the construction of harmonious and sustainable human development.

On the threshold of the 21st century, forward management implies new policies and new paradigms for higher education founded on such concepts as anticipatory capacity. Among other things, it is necessary 'to render more dynamic the reform of the study programmes, introducing flexible new mechanisms in order to satisfy in advance the needs and requirements of the labour sector. More generally, it is necessary to adopt organizational structures and education strategies enabling them to respond with both the timeliness and anticipation needed to creatively and efficiently face an uncertain future. In line with the universality of higher education, forward management must concern itself with universal ethics, that is, with providing guidance in value crises.

While the concept of quality control suits a closed production system in which intervention by individuals plays a minor role, it is inappropriate in an open system where human resources play a decisive role. The core of the management system must be the more open concept of quality assessment or evaluation. Quality control implies that the products of the system can be described unambiguously and indisputably by means of exact, pre-determinable indicators.

Quality assessment implies that the parties involved get together and agree on quality criteria. Some of these criteria can be converted into observable indicators, while others resist such attempts; certain criteria are sufficiently comprehensive to be usable at different times and places, while others are specific to a certain category of contexts or to clearly circumscribed periods; some criteria describe the products expected, others relate to required conditions or to processes to be employed (e.g. required qualifications, use of teaching resources, evaluation of teaching practices, etc) . In every case, what characterizes quality assessment is the active participation of all parties concerned, who together analyse a body of relevant, valid and reliable data before taking decisions aimed at improving and not simply at penalizing.

A task-oriented management system centred on the quest for quality and relevance implies that everyone involved in a higher-education institution should resist the temptation to withdraw to a reliance on selfish or corporatist freedoms, to reject transparency and accountability and to distrust certain of the institution's bodies or components. It is essential to link the concepts of responsible autonomy and accountability in order to recast the concept of academic freedom, whose meaning has frequently been distorted with the passage of time by withdrawal mechanisms.

A higher-education institution has an observation and consciousness-raising function. As a global system interacting with an external environment which can exert all sorts of pressures, for example regarding financing, its freedom must be viewed in the following terms: external authorities are responsible for defining a development policy on the basis of a set of relevant data (some of which may be the outcome of work done in higher education) and for consulting the higher-education institutions concerning their exact tasks; once these tasks have been clarified, the institutions must demand and safeguard their autonomy and responsibility for the way in which they discharge their tasks, given their available resources; but the institutions have a simultaneous duty to report on the results of their actions according as they tie in with the tasks set and the resources provided, just as the external authorities are required to account for the results of their policies (choice of priorities according to a development context not just here and now but also in the future).

A higher-education institution is a set of sub-systems. Analysis of numerous case studies of management models highlights two major and opposing models: a highly centralized and a highly decentralized model. There is a mean between the two which is showing increasing signs of developing in universities which are attempting to adapt to the changes occurring in the world. In the centralized model, the intermediate structures (usually faculties and departments) are convenient administrative ways of subdividing a sprawling whole into logical subsystems based nearly always on disciplines, but they derive their power from the central authorities in regard not only to important decisions but also in many cases to minor ones (for example, permission to send a fax or providing paper for a photocopier). This model still persists in some institutions, particularly in certain developing countries. In the decentralized model, intermediate structures are highly autonomous and therefore possess great independence, so that neighbouring departments may operate very differently. Here the central authorities act mainly as the representative of the institution as a whole with respect to external institutions or on ceremonial occasions.

Particularly when pushed to extremes, both these models fail to meet the requirements of universal higher education. The centralized model tends to produce people who simply obey orders and does not stimulate the observation and consciousness-raising function of every member of the institution (students, teachers/ researchers, blue-collar and white-collar staff), this task being left to the central authorities. The decentralized model tends to place the various functions side by side rather than create a coherent whole which serves the tasks of the global institution ('the whole is not the sum of the parts'); it also tends to cling to particular characteristics, corporatist attitudes and traditional rigidities. To deal with the changes, we must therefore introduce a third way: autonomous, responsible and accountable intermediate structures together with strong professional central authorities.

This management model emerges particularly clearly from the case studies analysed at the Palermo Regional Conference. Central levels of the university will need to be very effective in coherent strategic policy formation; redistribution of resources on strategic lines; evaluation and monitoring via improved information systems; searching for big external business and providing sensitive support to faculties. The central level also has an important part to play in relations with the local, regional and international levels. For example, it has to play a negotiating or even a lobbying role with respect to government authorities, in order not only to safeguard its autonomy of thought and action whilst remaining accountable but also to play its part as a universal university, for example its function of observation and consciousness-raising, its duty to contribute to harmonious and sustainable human development, its concern to be able to manage student and staff flows according to the principles of merit and equity, etc.

Higher education is facing a heavy expansion which will continue increasing under the combined effect of two factors: population growth and the demand for ever-higher levels of education. There has been an increase worldwide in higher-education enrolment rates between 1985 and 1995. This trend will probably continue, as the demand for higher educational levels is very strong. There has been a reduction worldwide in the imbalance between enrolment rates for girls and boys, but this imbalance has not yet disappeared, particularly in certain regions, as will be seen. In the developed countries, enrolment rates rose considerably between 1985 and 1995 . This trend will continue, as the question of educational level is important both to families and to policymakers, despite an ageing population.

In the developed countries, enrolment rates for girls now exceed those for boys. More refined statistics by course of study show, however, that the majority of them take arts and human sciences courses. In the developing regions, higher-education enrolment rates are markedly lower than in the developed countries. The gap has widened in 10 years, the increase in enrolment rates in the developing regions being less marked than in the developed regions. However, in actual numbers, the developing regions enrolled more students in 1995 than the developed countries, while it was the reverse in 1985. This is due to heavy population growth: young people represent an ever greater part of the population even if the projections show a decrease in the level of economic dependency as a result of improved life expectancy. In the developing regions, the sub-Saharan African region gives cause for particular concern because it has the lowest enrolment rates. Its situation is fairly similar to that of the least advanced countries.

Higher education is facing an increase in enrolments both in percentages and in actual numbers, a demand for higher educational levels which will continue increasing in every region of the world and an increasing number of enrolments of girls, accompanied however by imbalances between regions and the sexes. Side by side with this extremely strong demand resulting from educational expansion, higher education has simultaneously to cope with an increasing demand for quality services of various kinds.

The regional conferences were agreed on stressing the state's obligations to education in general and to higher education in particular. 'Governments must guarantee that the right to education is fulfilled. Consequently, they must take up the responsibility of financing education within the framework and conditions and demands that are typical of each educational system. Public support for higher education is still indispensable. The challenges faced by higher education are also challenges for society as a whole. Governments and Parliaments must fulfil their commitments to higher education and be accountable for pledges made at regional and world conferences over the past decade with regard to the provision of human and financial resources.

There is currently even a tendency inspired by certain neo-liberal theories to reduce the state's financial obligations towards higher education by invoking a certain interpretation of the concept of 'education-derived income', i.e. the direct or indirect benefits generated by education. The argument advanced by promoters of this tendency may be summarized as follows: the human capital generated by higher education is particularly large and graduate students are the principal beneficiaries;

their training has provided them with a culture and professionalism which distinguish them sharply from unqualified or less qualified persons, which provide them with greater productivity and therefore with markedly higher incomes which are ultimately due to the higher-education training received.

The proponents of this idea claim that it is unjust that financing should come in the main from the community, i.e. mainly from those who do not benefit from it. In their view, this is particularly unjust because the poorest pay proportionately more tax than the wealthiest and are the ones who benefit from it the least. These same proponents accordingly advocate a reduction of state participation in the financing of higher education in favour of a quest for alternatives whereby those benefiting from higher education would make a greater financial contribution.

This interpretation is hotly disputed by many economists who have examined the concept of income derived from education, especially from higher education. Thus, in the opinion of Hidalgo , 'knowledge is not a taxable base... and education-derived income does not emerge from the education system, it is external to it. ... This income is not expressed in the training process of the student, but in:

(a) the personal income of the trainee that joins the labour market;

(b) the productivity increase of the party incorporating the trainee to the process for the production of goods and services;

(c) the productivity increase of those who directly and indirectly incorporate technical and scientific progress;

(d) the productivity increase of the system as a whole resulting from the technical progress incorporated and the work qualification derived from the educational offer of the university'.

The education-derived income which benefits the individual should be replaced by the concept of external economy and particularly by the concept of social profitability, which denotes the indirect benefits generated by education for society. These benefits are difficult to quantify but are nonetheless real: the increased level of knowledge and skill has an impact on a country's growth rate and competitiveness; investments made by previous generations benefit later generations; the skills of those with ability (the concept of merit) can be put to optimum use in the service of development; the raised educational level has an effect on the development of a more democratic culture and allows distancing from, and resistance to, arbitrary acts and attitudes.

Payment of fees is undoubtedly one of the most frequently mentioned sources of financing. It can take various forms: 'direct' payment (lump sum or payment in instalments to ease the burden) by the student or family for a degree course or one or more individual courses; tuition loans or financing for full or partial reimbursement (there are many different schemes); mixed schemes. The practice of charging fees to the student or family concerned does not exist only in private institutions; although always controlled, it has become general practice in many public universities, especially in the developed countries; amounts vary greatly from country to country.

While the issue of fees was much discussed by the regional conferences, the arguments against are distinctly more numerous and more frequently invoked than those in favour. The arguments advanced in favour of fees are mainly the following:

(a) the needs which higher education must satisfy are extremely and increasingly numerous, and it is difficult for governments to find all the resources needed to meet them;

(b) higher education offers graduates appreciable benefits of various kinds (financial, social, cultural);

(c) payment of fees increases motivation;

(d) cost consciousness leads to a heightened awareness of the need for effectiveness and efficiency;

(e) differentiated fee structures are an aid to the diversification of higher education both within and among institutions.

The arguments against fees can be summarized as follows:

(a) the importance of higher education for a country's development needs no further demonstration and the state, which is responsible for framing development policy, therefore cannot evade its obligation to give priority to the financing of higher education;

(b) although individuals benefit, higher-education investment transcends the individual and represents an investment for the future;

(c) motivation should not depend on financial incentives;

(d) fees are not a pre-condition for greater effectiveness

and efficiency, quality-assessment strategies being much more relevant and necessary;

(e) it is not reasonable to charge fees during periods of economic recession; higher education is, on the contrary, an investment in research and training which will eventually make it possible to find a definitive solution to the crisis;

(f) in the developing countries, most families are unable to pay even minimal fees;

(g) numerous studies show that charging fees reduces access to higher education and leads to greater social inequity.

Despite their awareness that the question of student participation in the cost of studies could not be postponed indefinitely, the regional conferences reiterated that access to higher education should be based on merit and that this criterion outweighed all others; policies on fees should therefore give this criterion priority over all others, even if it meant introducing positive-discrimination arrangements (scholarships, reduced charges etc). The situation in certain states is particularly worrying, especially in sub-Saharan Africa. 'It is unrealistic to expect that African governments will in fact improve higher education funding in real terms'. What routes should therefore be followed? The proposals mentioned include:

(a) encouraging cheaper forms of higher education (shorter, more highly targeted courses employing some hourly-paid professional teachers and providing links between courses in order to enable students to change subjects or levels);

(b) establishing teaching arrangements not involving the on-campus costs which burden developing-country budgets (distance learning, decentralization of training, use of IT, provided the costs are carefully studied and a distinction made between investment costs and recurring costs);

(c) creating regional or international networks in order not to duplicate expensive types of training in every institution and country and to provide higher-quality or less expensive education by establishing centres of excellence and distributing them at the regional or international level (although this implies open agreements and respect by each partner for its commitments);

(d) obtaining the support of business and industry through sponsorships, grants and also access to various facilities;

(e) in partnership with the world of work, selling training courses as part of lifelong training policy;

(f) offering to the world of work, or to government, productive activities (services, consultancies, expertise, research) or production goods (agricultural or industrial products, development of new technologies) and to this end establishing a management structure for such activities so as to make them profitable to the university whilst simultaneously involving the relevant teachers/researchers;

(g) developing coherent – and not scattered – co-operation policies in order to optimize the not insignificant resources which are garnered through these channels;

(h) creating where possible associations of former students who will interest themselves in directly or indirectly supporting the institution which has trained them, along the lines of the associations existing in certain countries.

Management of Cooperartion in Higher Education

Today we are witnessing processes of internationalization and globalization in all fields. Caught in the grip of the prevailing economic liberalism, markets are becoming global: many trade transactions take place without the goods being seen or touched by middlemen; capital is circulating more quickly than individuals; businesses relocate according to the ebb and flow of advantage; highly skilled human resources are becoming increasingly mobile; the competition to win contracts demands an ever-higher level of skill in lowering costs and improving quality. But this frenzied race to achieve an ever better and cheaper product reaching the greatest possible number of people relies on the dependence of economies on the applications of advanced knowledge and research and thus on higher education.

Society is becoming increasingly a knowledge society and therefore increasingly dependent on the quality of higher education and its openness to the outside world. Globalization is bringing regionalization in its train. To become more competitive, states are federating and are developing policies of economic, monetary, political and even cultural integration. Large free-trade zones are being created, e.g. the European Common Market (which signs agreements with certain sub-Mediterranean countries), NAFTA, which groups together Mexico, the United States and Canada, and MERCOSUR (Argentina, Brazil, Paraguay and Bolivia). In Asia, many countries are signing co-operation agreements under the aegis of APEC (Asia Pacific Co-operation). On every continent all sorts of groups are being created and agreements entered into. The latter have numerous repercussions in many other domains: joint defence agreements, joint monetary policies (e.g. creation of a common regional currency, such as the Euro), cultural agreements (exchanges of productions, creation and support of major regional television networks, regional cultural events), policies on the defence or promotion of a common language. There is a considerable call for higher education for these regionalization projects, as the numerous regional-level exchange programmes bear witness.

Paradoxically, globalization and regionalization have perverse effects which run counter to a policy of sustainable human development and which higher education cannot endorse:

— *Polarization*: certain regions of the world become attractive, others become the opposite; the principles of 'where it is cheapest' and 'where there is least risk' prevail over the principles of 'where the need is greatest' and 'where solidarity is necessary'.

— *Marginalization*: the gap is widening between poor and rich regions as a result of an exceedingly vicious circle; without solidarity, countries with less knowledge or less power are increasingly edged out of the race for knowledge which is the basis of power, since knowledge is increasing exponentially; even within the poorer regions, marginalization is taking hold in varying degrees depending on the presence or absence of 'troubles', depending on the type of political regime, the existence or otherwise of a culture of corruption, the level of education.

— *Fragmentation*: driven by the perfectly legitimate need to seek an identity and faced with the juggernaut of globalization and the ensuing cultural and linguistic hegemonies, many social groups are endeavouring to assert a common identity on the basis of shared characteristics (ethnic group, territory, religion, rite, custom, culture, race) and of exclusion mechanisms which enable them, in their view, to assert their identity more strongly; the result is a withdrawal into policies of ethnicization, religious fundamentalism, closing of borders and cultural extremism.

Both globalization which benefits only the strong and polarization, marginalization and fragmentation are policies which act as a brake on sustainable human development and a culture of peace. Co-operation cannot serve such policies. While we certainly need a knowledge society, we also need a society of interdependent citizens: that is the basic principle of true co-operation.

The massive arrival of the new information and communication technologies has many consequences for the world of work: decision-making is increasingly remote from areas of production; it can be carried out in real time thousands of kilometres away; IT makes possible all sorts of remote consultation (stock exchanges, business-health indicators, lists of potential customers, lists of sub-contractors, price indexes etc); money no longer circulates in cash or paper but in virtual form; bookkeeping is becoming increasingly delocalized; areas of production, distribution and research are becoming increasingly separate geographically but increasingly linked by the new technology; as early as the stage of design the large collocated groupings are structured into sub-units which are autonomous but organized both into internal networks and into external networks linked to more flexible SMF sub-contractors; to enhance this flexibility, new structures are being created or further developed, such as temporary employment agencies, human-resource centres, auditing companies and services, recruitment companies, accountancy centres; thanks to information technology teleworking is becoming easier and new work-scheduling policies are being tried out. The coming of this communication society also brings with it numerous implications for the world of culture.

Because of the new communication technologies, more and more individuals have simultaneous access to the same information and have the impression of living in a 'global village'. Information technology is therefore both a vehicle for the internalization of culture and a tool for defending cultural identity: a major challenge to which higher education cannot remain indifferent. Higher education is closely linked to the world of work and of culture: it trains the experts and develops the advanced knowledge which the world of work needs; it is the repository of universal culture and contributes to its creation.

Higher-education institutions cannot remain aloof from the IT without detracting from the performance of their various teaching, research and service tasks; in fact, they should take a part in its development and anticipate the consequences of its application in the different sectors, and thus first of all for themselves. These potential consequences for higher education are many and various. At the same time there is a risk of a type of higher education developing which will be increasingly heterogeneous and inegalitarian, to the benefit of the already highly developed countries and to the detriment of the least-developed countries. The challenge for higher education is whether it will allow the vicious circle of under-development to speed up under the effects of the inegalitarian development of IT or whether it is prepared to take up the gauntlet by establishing without delay a network covering all countries and by making a considerable effort, taking precedence over all else, on behalf of the developing countries. The choice lies between a policy of marginalization, and therefore of domination and subjection, and a policy of solidarity and partnership.

In recent decades the model that has explicitly or implicitly dominated many co-operation policies has been rooted in the idea that economic considerations are the basis for development and thus for co-operation. This idea has led to the following approaches:

— Priority has been given to sectors yielding a high immediate economic return (e.g. the exploitation of mineral or food resources) and providing the donor countries with large profits. The co-operation projects of those countries formed part of a profitable overall commercial policy; however, for the developing countries, the preferential support given to certain sectors often led eventually to imbalances in their system as a whole, particularly at the moment when the donors decided to withdraw. The approach to this type of co-operation bears all the hallmarks of dependency: the sectors to be covered by the co-operation programmes are chosen by the donors or lenders; the sums involved are often determined before needs have been analysed with the partners; projects are often short-term ones in which no account is taken of the consequences and costs to the beneficiary country of a halt in the project; lenders distinguish not between good and bad borrowers but rather between docile and non-docile borrowers;

— The 'co-operation market' is shared mainly between a number of major fund providers, namely the international banks and the bilateral co-operation agencies which have historical links with the countries concerned;

— Co-operation projects and programmes are often identified on the basis of vague and incomplete information and analysis: information sources are often external (i.e. coming from abroad); when they are internal, they are often manipulated to conform with the criteria set by the lender or donor; the latter often tries to devise a homogeneous approach and procedure which can be used uniformly for differing situations; this attitude is often geared more closely to policies and politicians than to the projects themselves, their performance, reimbursement capacity or the ability to pursue them.

The polarization of co-operation based on economic considerations explains the small share devoted by the developed countries to education in general and higher education in particular. According to Hallak again, this share does not exceed 1 per cent of their GDP. In the case of the development banks, investment in education is the smallest of all investments.

In view of the tiny amount devoted to education, a dilemma tends to appear as between higher education and basic education to the detriment of the former, with no one asking about the reasons for the smallness of the funds for the education system as a whole or bearing in mind that the various education and information levels cannot be separated. Historically the developed countries helped to create higher education in their regions of influence in order to train efficient managers. Their policy was to complete co-operation in higher education and then terminate it (very largely or even almost totally) as soon as the higher-education system as a whole was close enough to a carbon copy of the organization in the home country and enough local graduates had been trained.

The developing countries therefore found themselves with 'complete' institutions (which is what they originally wanted), and with teachers/researchers trained mostly in the countries of the North to deal with problems which concerned the latter countries but which were not necessarily relevant or important for their country of origin. Faced with the expansion in education and the financial crisis of 1997-98, the higher-education institutions of the developing countries have found themselves accepting large numbers of students in traditional subjects who hoped that their diplomas would always be a passport to a job in the civil service. The system created job-seekers and not job-creators at a time when the countries had enormous, and changing, needs.

While tertiary training was becoming increasingly restricted to the country of origin, certain developed countries attracted and still attract the best brains of the developing countries or students from prosperous backgrounds. In 1995, the USA received 453,787 foreign students, who represented 30.2 per cent of their student population, France received 170,574, i.e. 11.4 per cent,

Germany 146,126, i.e. 9.7 per cent and the United Kingdom 128,550 or 8.6 per cent. All these countries experienced a substantial growth in their student numbers between 1985 and 1995. In the Asia-Pacific zone, a similar pattern has emerged with regard to Japan and Australia, with an annual growth of 19.2 and 12.9 per cent respectively between 1985 and 1995. China is now experiencing the same trend: the number of its foreign students rose from 3,000 in 1986 to 23,000 in 1993, an annual growth rate of 27 per cent. Many students from developing countries are therefore to be found in the research laboratories of the developed countries, and many of them stay there.

It is therefore not surprising that the vast majority of data bases are developed in those countries, that the vast majority of patents relate to those same countries and that 80 per cent of technological transfers are still from those countries. All this is caused by the brain drain; the countries of origin receive little return on this investment. The vicious circle of under-development accordingly becomes ever more marked.

The most pressing need for international co-operation in higher education is to reverse the process of decline of institutions in the developing countries, particularly in the least developed. The adverse conditions in which higher education has to function call, first of all, for appropriate measures and efforts by the respective states and institutions. They must learn to be more effective and efficient in strengthening their links with society so as to play a full part in the development efforts of their region or community. It is not unusual to perceive the university-level establishment as part of the institutional machinery of the state instead of seeing it as an essential part of a local community and of society in general. It is essential to persuade the decision-makers and all of society that the latter is the case

For the construction of sustainable human development and a culture of peace, we must therefore advocate a logic of co-operation based on the interdependence of all societal components and on solidarity in the struggle against imbalances and the vicious circle of underdevelopment. This new logic implies a quest for harmonization between the world of work and the other components of society and, accordingly, harmonization between the world of work and higher education in a spirit of partnership. There is one fixed basic principle: higher-education institutions must not set their long-term guidelines exclusively in the light of the labour market or of forward studies of labour requirements but of social needs.

The world of work helps to create wealth that can be reinvested to meet the other needs of society but, in a society which is becoming increasingly knowledge-based, it has an increasing need for staff with high technical qualifications but a humanist view of the pursuit of their activities and an ability to anticipate future needs and requirements, especially those connected with constructing a more just society.

For its part, higher education cannot loftily ignore the fact that the world of work and the whole of society are evolving ever more rapidly. If it is not to fail in its fundamental task, it must therefore make a point of establishing partnerships with the world of work in order to supply the needs of its training programmes in accordance with the rapid advance in knowledge, develop in those programmes the skills needed by society in general and the world of work in particular, create an entrepreneurial spirit and pave the way for professional and cultural mobility. Such harmonization also implies that higher education must adapt its training structures and arrangements to the new needs or create new forms of teaching on the basis of criteria such as flexibility, employability, adaptation to a wide variety of contexts and publics, the principle of life-long training and the internationalization of training.

The task is therefore to change from a paradigm centred on teaching and the transmission of knowledge to one centred on learning and the development of transferable skills in differing space and time contexts. A wide range of approaches and schemes will therefore be necessary: modularization together with a precise definition of the initial skills demanded and the skills required on graduation, capitalization, allowance for life experience, networking of training courses, diversification of subjects with greater use of short professional courses, establishment of 'bridges' between training courses, use of common differentiated standards, accreditation and recognition of qualifications, distance learning, types of supervision based on decentralization or the use of IT, diversification of institutions and courses, work experience.

These changes entail several levels of co-operation:

— co-operation with the world of work (production, service and creative enterprises, including the SMEs and the community service arrangements which are generating an increasing number of jobs) by jointly defining relevant training policies, collaborating and exchanging resources for certain training modules, supplying expertise, taking part in studies of the labour market and changes in needs, evaluating alternative scenarios, seeking out and developing new technologies or transferring knowledge and studying the social and ecological impact of certain choices;

— internal co-operation between higher-education institutions at both the national and regional levels according to the following principles: quality, effectiveness and efficiency requirements are such that not every institution can organize all training programmes or maintain research laboratories whose resources are quantitatively and qualitatively sufficient in all sectors; the organization of distance-learning schemes increasingly means that a regional outlook must be cultivated for cost reasons and in order to strengthen integration policies;

— co-operation at international level based both on solidarity and respect for differences in order to provide a relevant and equitable answer to the challenges of globalization and internationalization; this implies a policy of quality which, when applied, will take into account the specific features of the contexts ('think globally and act locally'); provision of data bases in all countries, including the least developed; post-graduate and post-doctorate courses under international programmes and in collaboration with centres of excellence, with the dual aim of acquiring qualifications which are both of an extremely high level and applicable to the situation in the country of origin; co-operation policies which allow the developing countries to get something back from the benefits derived by the most developed countries from the brain drain; international-co-operation actions designed to eradicate crucial problems such as hunger, disease, illiteracy, environmental destruction, violence and marginalization.

This harmonization between the world of work and higher education is a two-way process: not only must changes in the world of work in a changing society compel higher education to make its training more relevant and to support development through its research, but higher education in its turn must urge the world of work to reform itself so as to promote sustainable human development and a culture of peace.

Higher education must discharge its duties of observation, consciousness-raising and anticipation in this context, too, by standing back and looking at society in the round. Here too, higher education must not simply provide training but must also produce citizens who are aware of their own individual surroundings and of the society of which they are members. This is the context in which regional and international cultural co-operation must be visualized in order not only to preserve and disseminate the different heritages but also to create a culture of peace, conceived as a world which has been liberated from all conflict and enjoys evenly-distributed socio-economic prosperity, enriched by cultural diversity and a common concern to create a democratic society.

In this knowledge society the workforce is increasingly becoming a cognitive force; capital is increasingly becoming a capital of advanced knowledge and of skills in solving problems and finding new solutions; we have entered the information and communication era; the international dimension is present everywhere. Implementing this new co-operation policy therefore depends in the main on creating networks between higher education and its partners. Organizing or strengthening networks and establishing local, national, regional and international links between them should be one of higher education's priority tasks.

In this context it is important to identify some basic guidelines for implementing this new policy:

(i) Internationalization and networking call for much study and for agreements on comparable standards not only of communication but also of quality. This involves many fields: the introduction of regional and international teaching and research programmes; the creation of centres of excellence; the recognition of studies and qualifications; the mobility of students, teachers, researchers and managers; the employability of professionals working in a variety of professional, social and cultural contexts.

(ii) At the same time, the strengthening of regional and international programmes implies awareness at local level of the regional, international and global implications of most of the questions which local and national communities must confront. The networking of higher-education managers is a contribution to this end and should be stepped up as it is becoming an unavoidable necessity.

(iii) The new information and communication technologies will play an increasingly important role in co-operation, as pointed out by the regional conferences, particularly Beirut. But in some places what is realistic and socially possible is much more limited. The Dakar Regional Conference spoke for the poor countries when it said: 'There are many obstacles to be overcome in the developing countries:

the small existing number of potential users possessing both the capability and equipment to benefit from access to electronic information networks; the scarcity and expensiveness of equipment, software and information in comparison with the North; the lack of accessible telecommunications infrastructure; telecommunications monopolies together with over-regulation and high cost; the uncertainty of electricity supply in many countries; the lack of interregional networks and co-operation. Over and beyond the purely technical and material aspects, one of the major conditions for introducing such facilities lies in the supplying of computers with suitable, meaningful and sufficiently good educational messages'. It is important to accept the challenge in order not to worsen the vicious circle of under-development. Addressing this challenge should be a priority task of co-operation.

(iv) Distance learning and the virtual university are certainly facilities which must be given priority in the context of co-operation because they enable internationalization and networking to be put into practice. Virtual-world models help the student to visualize complex structures not permitted by text, videos or other graphic models; they also allow experiments which are not feasible in the real world. Such facilities should, however, be viewed in the framework of co-operation based not on an exclusive model of exporting training or franchised schemes but on integration into a local context and partnership with local actors.

(v) The academic mobility of students, teachers, researchers and managers must be increased. Many experiments have been carried out on the various continents and lessons must be drawn from them. The main difficulties which must be resolved include: academic years do not always correspond; even where agreements exist, the transfer of funds is sometimes hindered by a lack of confidence; the length of courses varies from one institution to another; procedures for immigration and visas are sometimes lengthy and inquisitorial and hold up the travel arrangements of the persons concerned; language proficiency is still too often inadequate; funding is inadequate; participants often deplore the lack of information; individuals with families are not always prepared to leave their countries for fairly long periods. These difficulties require the persons responsible for managing mobility policy to get together at regional level. To make mobility attractive and effective, it is suggested that: (a) the profile of exchanges be raised, drawing attention to the benefits; (b) that governments and the private sector be urged to strengthen financial support for exchange policies; (c) that flexibility be strengthened by developing guidelines which will reflect the great diversity of systems and cultures.

(vi) Some people consider that, as the multinational companies play an important part in internationalization, they should be called upon to assume their responsibilities and assist with the training of higher-education graduates from the developing countries. Co-operation projects linking those companies and higher education should therefore set themselves the goal of training highly qualified professionals who would then be able to take over jobs often assigned to staff from developed countries. Likewise, as multinationals frequently work on a sub-contract basis with SMFs, co-operation projects could target the development of an entrepreneurial attitude in people capable of setting up small businesses to meet unsatisfied needs. Higher-education institutions could also involve themselves in the creation of science parks to bring together small and large companies with a high added value in terms of knowledge development, new technology and knowledge transfer. Support for graduates in creating their own jobs is therefore an important objective of co-operation. A close look should be taken at the experience of the co-operative banks and the Grameen Bank initiative in Bangladesh.

It is essential for intergovernmental, governmental and non-governmental bodies concerned with development and its funding, and also the academic community, in general, to consider the higher-education institutions of the developing countries as playing an essential role in the overall development of the education system and the promotion of endogenous capacities. This calls for co-ordinated forward management of co-operation. This can be defined in terms of a number of lines of study and action:

(i) One of the major objectives of international co-operation is therefore '...the strengthening of the key components of integration and the co-ordination of the subjects, institutions, agencies and resources to guarantee a type of shared horizontal co-operation and avoid substituting, altering or directing the local initiative'

(ii) A relevant policy and an overall action plan must have been defined in consultation with the various partners and on the basis of an analysis of past or present experience, anticipation of their side-effects and the new priority challenges to be faced. This is the primary and basic approach of all co-ordinated forward management.

(iii) International co-operation must be able to assist managers to define their co-operation policy and translate it into a plan of action by organizing meetings to exchange experience and analyse case studies. This is particularly important in the case of relatively new initiatives such as distance learning or networking.

(iv) In addition to ad hoc evaluations, co-ordinated forward management needs to be based on permanent 'observatories' of society's key components and on future studies in order to guide co-operation.

(v) At every stage from design to evaluation, including implementation, co-operation must be served by genuine experts. If we are not to return to an outdated pattern of co-operation, it is important not only to restate that local co-operation circles (administrators, co-ordinators and promoters) bear the main responsibility for designing, formulating and implementing proposals for change but also to rely on local experts in the different project phases.

(vi) To be effective, co-operation projects need competent and well-trained managers. Co-operation therefore begins with 'programmes for the training of senior, middle-level and potential managers of higher

> education' who not only possess a thorough knowledge of the rules and instruments of good and effective management but who are also aware that it is important to 'lay a basis for self-reliance and avoid excessive dependence on external funding because real development can only come from within'. Consequently, 'co-operation and partnerships should be equitable, based on dialogue, consensus and respect for each partner rather than on donor/sponsor power'.

The World Conference on Higher Education is called upon to make a strong plea in favour of further promoting the internationalization of higher education and of identifying ways and means whereby this process can be made more effective, efficient and equitable for all. A second challenge concerns the growing complexity of international co-operation. Originally limited to the mobility of individuals, which has now found an effective instrument in the regional conventions on the recognition of higher-education studies and qualifications, it now assumes a broad range of forms, particularly through various types of networking and linking arrangements among institutions, academics and students.

Co-operation must be seen as part and parcel of the institutional mission of higher-educational institutions and systems; it must increasingly employ networking and responsibility-sharing and have solidarity as the basic principle for an improved sharing of knowledge. Co-operation therefore depends on a wider spectrum of expertise and on management which, being future-oriented and co-ordinated, is more professional. New forms of co-operation are emerging; they demand great creativity in order to plan them, technical skill in order to master them, realism in order to implement them effectively and efficiently, and discussion and impartiality in order to evaluate them and anticipate their future. Higher education has therefore an important role to play in co-operation, but it must be aware of the stakes first of all for itself, secondly for the other educational levels and finally for the overall development of society.

6

Gender Issues in Higher Education

The key dimensions of human development have become: empowerment, co-operation, equity, sustainability and security. The commitment to these goals by the family of world nations can only be possible if effective partnerships are formed to construct a more human society in order to realize the potential of investment in human capital and co-operative action. This emphasis on dialogue, on coalition and on collaboration forms the basis of the new approach to development strategy and requires full participation from the relevant actors involved - that is to say, from men and wome. The 4th World Conference on Women merits special attention for its role as a watershed in the history of women's social empowerment and leadership: firstly, it confirmed that the entire gender issue has gained worldwide attention as a crucial component in the development process; with this recognition, it may be possible to redress the inequalities more effectively: secondly, and compared with earlier conferences, it resulted in more concrete recommendations to help ensure that women take their full place in the world of the 21st century.

Many of the key problems faced by women and identified in the Beijing Declaration remain unsolved: persistent poverty, inequality of access to education, health and welfare, violence, impact of armed conflicts, absence from decision-making in the economic sector, unequal participation in the power structures of society, insufficient mechanisms to promote the advancement of women, inadequate recognition of women's rights, failure to recognize women's contribution to society, insufficient recognition of their contribution to environmental protection and management. These problems impede the personal and social empowerment of women, and, consequently, they hinder their ability to emerge as effective leaders at every level of daily life.

While progress has been significant, much remains to be done as is evidenced by statistics stated in Human Development Report published annually by the United Nations Development Programme:

— 66% of the world's illiterates are women;

— only 33% of women compared to men enrol in higher education in Sub-Saharan Africa with even lower figures in science and technology;

— their participation in employment is only 50% compared to that of men in developing countries;

— women in certain countries still cannot vote or own property;

— in politics they represent only 10% of the world's parliamentarians;

— national GNPs could rise significantly if women's unpaid work was an official factor in production;

— women still suffer salary disparity compared to men in numerous instances of professional life.

Clearly rapid change must occur and the role of education, notably as an investment in human capital, is an essential aspect of this challenge where men and women have equal responsibility. Against this background, the thorough and far-reaching renovation of education systems has gained considerable support as one effective way to tackle social problems - old and new.

These issues of women in higher education dominated in the 1994 Policy Papers entitled *Higher Education: The Lessons of Experience and Higher Education for Change and Development*, prepared respectively by the World Bank and UNESCO. With regard to the major challenges facing higher education in various regions of the world, it is possible to propose the following summaries:

— in Africa, the continuing development problems and donor insistence on basic education, has deflected attention from higher learning which, as the globalization phenomenon gathers momentum, risks its further decline. There is now a strong dynamic towards renewal to be considered as a partner, rather than a dependent, in a new social order. The gender issue in higher education has emerged as a top priority in this region;

— the Arab States are marked by great cultural diversity, economic disparities and social instability. Here, since populations are numerous and very young, there is an urgent need to modernize systems and structures to meet the demand for higher education and to help shape a more stable society. Currently, women are very rare as leaders in higher education institutions;

— Asia and the Pacific is the region which has experimented most widely with higher education - very often to meet the new employment requirements of market-driven economies. In contrast, serious poverty persists in certain countries and an over-supply of academic graduates (notably in India) face problems of employment in rapidly changing job markets. Gender is approached in many different ways in this culturally diverse region - however, women as heads of institutions are few.

— Europe, of course, encompasses countries with vastly different systems and levels of development. Western European nations are currently engaged in wide-ranging reforms designed to attune higher education to a future society where key aspects such as employment and technology are undergoing radical transformation. Eastern and Central Europe, which are gearing their economies to the market system, have accelerated the modernization of higher education in an effort to equip their populations with the capacities necessary for the management of the social and economic transition in progress. Numerically, this region would have the highest instance of women in leadership posts;

— Latin America and the Caribbean, a basically rich region where social and economic stability has significantly improved, has a history of academic higher education with a strong tradition for private institutions. It is now committed to higher education which optimizes human capital and natural resources, thus re-orienting it to meet development priorities and the growing role of the region in the global economy.

Women are frequently present in management positions but the gender dimension must be treated with caution in certain contexts. Against this background, three specific aspects related to higher education and women emerge:

— firstly, women graduates must be seen as part of the essential human resource base of each country. As such they have then right to the same access and career opportunities as their male counterparts. Discriminatory practices are not only unjust but a flagrant wastage of valuable expertise which, today, is vital for all nations;

— secondly, in higher education itself where reform is the priority, there should be a strong commitment to equipping women with the necessary range of managerial skills to contribute to the overall renewal of this sector;

— thirdly, the nature of power, as it is used in positions of leadership and management, may need to be conceived quite differently. Feminine leadership needs clearer analysis and definition and may be preferred as a model more suited to the needs of social development across all sectors including, higher education.

Factors Affecting Women's Access to Higher Education

The factors are which are vital while considering women's access to higher education include:

— societal attitudes to women which discourage their participation in decision-making;

— their lower enrolments in higher education to date;

— the absence of a gender dimension in the higher education curriculum.

Participation in decision-making

Education facilitates empowerment which is essential for the participation of women in all aspects of the development process. Furthermore, higher education provides the expertise usually required for the key posts which shape policy in all fields - hence its particular importance for women is obvious. In the 1993, UNESCO/ Commonwealth Secretariat study entitled Women in Higher Education Management identified the principal barriers preventing the participation of women in the decision-making arena:

— limited access to education, especially higher education;

— discriminatory appointment and promotion practices;

— the stresses of dual family and professional roles;

— family attitudes;

— career interruptions;

— cultural stereotyping;

— alienation from the male culture and continued resistance to women in management positions;

— propagation of the glass ceiling syndrome which privileges covert criteria for advancement;

— absence of adequate policies and legislation to ensure the participation of women.

Given these obstacles, solutions to remedy the exclusion of women lie in a reversal of these trends by means of wider access to education, notably higher education, review of appointment and promotion procedures, provision of legislative and infra-structure support in all professions and of special programmes for women, affirmative action to favour women's access and participation while awaiting a genuine change in attitude towards full gender equality and institutional and governmental support through clear and effective policies which are actually enforced.

Enrolment Issues

The two decades have witnessed significant enrolment of the female population in higher education. This progress has certainly been due in part to specific strategies which have focused attention on the inequalities to be redressed. UN action has been effective in this regard as policy-makers have been sensitized to the rights of women and to the need to open all levels of education to their greater numbers.

A closer analysis of higher education statistics reveals the different nature of the problem in different socio-cultural and economic contexts. In general, women's enrolments have improved and may even exceed those of men. Moreover, certain countries have clearly made a strong commitment to facilitating the access of women to higher education.

Certain aspects of the access/ participation analysis require significant improvement, notably further analysis of the courses chosen by women, the fortunes of female graduates when they become predominant in a given profession yet fail to share in the decision-making process of that field, and the promotion of women in science at all levels of education so as to permit careers in this domain. From the economic standpoint, higher education qualifications effectively raise both employment prospects and social expectations of graduates.

Despite the current economic climate, those with a degree or diploma are ten times more likely to find employment that unskilled persons. Thus, it is high time to promote more enlightened attitudes towards highly educated women whose qualifications entitle them to career fulfilment and who - as the principal or equal salary-earner - require appropriate support in the management of personal and professional duties.

Gender dimension of curriculum

Gender dimension of the university curriculum can be justified on several counts:

- — recognition and enhancement of the university's role in society
- — the impact of Internationalization and Globalization
- — the creation and exchange of knowledge and know-how
- — the need to tackle social problems at the grass-roots level
- — mainstreaming of gender issues

In Women and the University Curriculum, produced to mark the 1995 Beijing Conference, the authors were in agreement that, today, the university curriculum must:

— offer stimulating role models for women students;

— encouragement and build their confidence

— present male-dominated careers in a light which is more attractive to women.

Moreover, since development theory acknowledges that the gender dimension has become a key factor in any solutions proposed for global problems, and as many higher education institutions are now engaged in far-reaching curriculum innovation to keep abreast of social change, the omission of this aspect is no longer acceptable.

Women's Leadership in Higher Education

We are at a certain point in the process of social change where management models are being questioned and where the numbers of women in various professional fields are increasing steadily. To some extent, this can be seen as a crossroads and the new direction taken is very important since this will lead to governance patterns in the 21st century. Current statistics from the world's principal associations of universities attest to the need to improve the presence of women at the top of higher education

As the challenges facing higher education grow more complex, it is true that the governance of this sector requires even greater skills. And, these challenges come at a time when top leadership itself is under close scrutiny. There is no reason why women should be excluded from this position of leadership and power, provided their capacities are those sought. First and foremost, this principle must be reiterated, accepted and practised in the field of higher education. Secondly, adequate training opportunities must be given to women to acquire skills which, otherwise, would exclude their candidature from consideration wnen leadership posts arise. For this reason, UNESCO, in co-operation with a number of NGOs promotes management capacities for higher education personnel - from VCs and rectors through the various echelons of the institutions. In particular, with the Association of Commonwealth Universities and the Commonwealth Secretariat, UNESCO has adopted a strategy to provide management training for women and research on the issues which can promote (or hinder) their advancement within the executive ranks. Topics covered include management development, Women's studies as a catalyst for their progress, the management of professional and personal roles, women and leadership and, from a broader standpoint, women and university governance.

In a world of increasing complexity, the quality of leadership has certainly assumed new proportions which are essential to the survival and success of any enterprise or institution. This brings us to the notion of feminine leadership and a number of related issues notably whether this is a valid concept and whether women will be permitted to claim their right to participation in higher education decision-making at all levels and on their own terms. In a study commissioned by UNESCO to the Inter-American Association for Higher Education, Professor Sheryl Bond of Queen's University, Canada, examined the concept of academic leadership today, emphasizing that the increasing appointment of women indicates the reality of social change. Factors preventing women's access to top positions are considered and new paradigms witnessing the interaction of social context and positional power are described. Bond advocates a move from debate to dialogue which will equate the advancement of women with the renewal and progress of the institution - an essential shift in thinking if higher education is to contribute effectively to the development process.

At the moment, feminine leadership and its possible benefits continue to constitute a controversial area of the debate in terms of empowerment for women. However, there is a growing belief that feminine leadership is emerging as a distinct force in management which has been influenced by very specific factors:

— a commitment to power sharing (which implies rejection of power by domination)

— an insistence on self-respect, service and the importance of merit

— a focus on concrete results in the professional context

— recognition and accommodation of the pressures of managing personal and professional lives.

As we continue in transition mode, a significant group would still deny these trends, insisting that access to decision-making still depends essentially on emulation of male behaviour.

The reality of cultural diversity is a most problematic area in relation to women as leaders and managers both in higher education and in society at large. Many factors come into play - the historical roles of women in certain societies, the conflicts arising from their advanced education and exposure to other cultures, their own continued commitment to the values of their own race, religion and nation. In dealing with the tension between women of varied cultures and their role in the advancement of higher education, several points must be kept in mind: the role of women in any given society is subject to a number of key traditions, some of which are age-old and must impact on their lives as citizens and professions in particularly complex ways; the Special Project Women, Higher Education and Development, by promoting the training and research modalities of the UNITWIN/UNESCO Chairs Programme, aims to improve the careers of women in priority areas such as higher education management, community health, social inclusion, poverty alleviation and science and development. These Chairs and networks recognize cultural identity as a key variable in structuring the activities implemented;

— in certain countries and cultures, highly women have had access to power but often because of their family, marital or political connections;

— management varies enormously amongst cultures

— a fact which has gained even greater attention with the reality of internationalization;

— an understanding of other peoples and of their languages as an expression of their thought patterns is now accepted as an essential component for successful enterprise in every sphere of activity;

— paradoxically, management is - universally - about getting things done by other people. Hence, at some point, it is essential for cultures to find common ground for dialogue and negotiation.

In the leadership and management of higher education, women of different cultures can network to exchange visions and views which enrich their own approaches to specific issues, including the way in which they handle male attitudes to power and decision-making in their own countries. Despite profound cultural diversity, certain precepts must guide women as they seek greater particiaption in decison-making and power sharing:

— Women's Legal Rights

— The Critical Mass Factor

— Adapting Cultural Traditions

— The Challenges of Leadership

— Institutional Commitment to Gender Equity

— Feminine Leadership

— The Social Responsibilities of Higher Education

These are universally valid and attest, in the most eloquent manner possible, to the feminine vision of priorities for higher education leadership in the coming years when a new social partnership will be increasing sought - not only by women but by all responsible citizens.

To promote advocacy concerning the access of women to higher education and their participation in this sector:

— International NGOs should undertake a critical review of legal instruments to ascertain effectiveness with regard to higher education

— NGOs, specialized or interested in women and higher education, should pursue training to perfect their advocacy skills in the field of gender at international, regional, national and institutional levels

— Via NGOs specialized in higher education (e.g. regional rectors' associations and conferences), a Charter of Commitment to Gender Equality should be drawn up for signature by institutional leaders

— Institutions should set up a senior committee to ensure that goals concerning gender equality are attained

— Equal Employment Opportunity Offices should be established in universities and higher education institutions to monitor the progress of women academics and administrators (e.g. appointment to chairs, HOD posts, senior management posts etc.)

— Career orientation offices and graduate placement services should adopt special measures to ensure that women students are fully informed of opportunities and obstacles with regard to gender in different professions

— Higher education institutions and NGOs should make optimal use of role models and pathfinders as a means to inform and advise women students concerning their career choices.

— A Code of Good Practice in each region should be elaborated to illustrate the promotion of gender equality across different cultural contexts

— NGOs specialized in higher education and women should run extensive training sessions for students and recent graduates, both men and women, on feminine leadership with a view to creating a more human society

— The principle of Lifelong Learning for women should be strongly supported and appropriate measures adopted to to permit them to continue their studies, to re-enter the workforce and to harmonize their professional and personal responsibilities.

7

Future Trends in Higher Education

Higher education's contribution to the economic and social well-being of a nation is of vital importance. Its research pushes back the frontiers of human knowledge and is the foundation of human progress.Its teaching educates and skills the youth for a knowledge-dominated age. It gives graduates both personal and intellectual fulfilment.Working with business,it powers the economy,and its graduates are crucial to the public services.And wide access to higher education makes for a more enlightened and socially just society. In a fast-changing and increasingly competitive world,the role of higher education in equipping the labour force with appropriate and relevant skills,in stimulating innovation and supporting productivity and in enriching the quality of life is central.

The universities and colleges have been through a dramatic transformation over the last quarter-century as participation in higher education has tripled,and generally have maintained high quality and good value despite a halving of the unit of funding. Universities also make a substantial contribution to the strength of the national economy. Links between universities and business are strong and growing. Record of the universities and colleges has been encouraging as measured by business start-ups and other spin out activity. In UK, during 2001,universities created 175 new spin-out companies,and that number has been increasing rapidly – it averaged around 70 a year in the five years to 1999 –2000. They include innovative companies like the Leeds spin-out Ecertec,which aims to develop smart materials that will allow,for example,'warpable ' wings to change shape on aircraft.

There has also been a sharp increase in the number of patents filed,up 22 per cent between 1998 –99 and 1999 –2000,and the proportion of higher education research income funded by companies in the UK is also up and is now at a higher level than even the USA.There are numerous examples of higher education institutions helping companies to be more innovative and competitive.For example,Exeter University provides product development facilities which have assisted more than 300 small firms.And institutions now offer a wide range of courses to provide continuing professional development to employees in specific firms or business sectors.

The universities have changed the nature of their provision to reflect the changing demands of students.Some higher education institutions have gone out of their way to encourage applications from schools and colleges whose students do not normally participate.Others have embraced new ways of delivering learning and new types of course to meet the needs of a wider range of learners.

Developed countries invest more in higher education institutions. France,Germany,the Netherlands UK, and USA all contribute 1 per cent of GDP in public funding to higher education institutions,and Japan is planning to increase public investment from 0.4 per cent to 1 per cent. The developing knowledge economy means the need for more,better trained people in the workforce.And higher education is becoming a global business.

The effect was particularly marked in institutions which were not research-intensive. Approximately half of the higher education estate was built,to relatively low and inflexible specifications,in the 1960s and early 1970s.Much of it is nearing the end of its design life, and new requirements arise from scientific and technological advance,as well as recent growth in research volumes.

Teaching has for too long been the poor relation in higher education.Promotion for academics is based largely on research excellence,rather than teaching ability.There is no respected and defined separate professional career track for higher education teaching in its own right.

Students have insufficient information on how good the teaching is when applying for courses.And here again there is a story of decline:staff-student ratios have fallen from just over 1:10 in 1983 to 1:18 in 2000 and this tends to mean that students write fewer assignments and have less face-to-face contact with staff. There is too little collaboration between higher education institutions (HEIs),which can raise standards;support the development of modules and courses particularly at the introductory level;and promote the innovative use of ICT and credit accumulation and transfer.

The proportion of businesses using information from HEIs to help with innovation has increased over recent years,and is now 16 per cent of companies.But this is still a small minority. When universities were asked to benchmark themselves,fewer than half declared that they had more than a restricted or partially implemented plan for business support.

Universities have often experienced difficulties in transferring knowledge to business through research and development work, and businesses are often unclear about what they want.And,though the new Regional Development Agencies are now building graduate-level skills into their planning,this is in many cases a relatively recent development.There is clearly scope for the higher education sector to improve its performance still further and for businesses to be clearer about what they want from HEIs.This will be informed by the outcome of the Lambert review,announced by the Chancellor ofthe Exchequer in November 2002,which will investigate ways in which the interactions between universities and businesses can be enhanced.

Demand for graduates is very strong,and research shows that 80 per cent of the 1.7 million new jobs which are expected to be created by the end of the decade will be in occupations which normally recruit those with higher education qualifications.

The pace of both social and technological change means that education, including higher education,can no longer be confined to the early years of life.This is truly an era of lifelong learning.Today 's generation of students will need to return to learning – full—time or part-time – on more that one occasion across their lifetime in order to refresh their knowledge,upgrade their skills and sustain their employability.Such independent learners investing in the continuous improvement of their skills will underpin innovation and enterprise in the economy and society.Lifelong learning therefore implies a fundamental shift from the 'once in a lifetime ' approach to higher education to one of educational progression linked to a process of continuous personal and professional development.

The skills gap is most acute at a level that is represented by higher education qualifications below degree level,particularly two-year work-focused provision. Jobs in the 'associate professional ' and higher technician level has experienced the greatest growth in the recent years, and the rate is increasing. In Uk analysis of the Employer Skills Survey 2002 shows that associate professionals and technical occupations have the highest proportion of skill shortage vacancies relative to the numbers employed – 1.2 per cent compared to 0.2 per cent for managers..Shorter,more work-focused courses are also better suited to a culture of continuous professional development. Work-focused courses at these levels have suffered from social and cultural prejudice against vocational education.Employers claim that they want graduates whose skills are better fitted for work;but the labour market premium they pay still favours traditional three-year honours degrees over two-year work-focused ones.And students have therefore continued to apply for three-year honours courses in preference.We must break this cycle of low esteem, to offer attractive choices to students about the types of course they can undertake.

Higher education should be a choice open to everyone with the potential to benefit – including older people in the workforce who want to update their skills.There are not enough choices for flexible study – including part—time courses, sandwich courses,distance learning,and e-learning – and there must be an increasingly rich variety of subjects to study,which keep pace with changes in society and the economy.

Universities are a vital gateway to opportunity and fulfilment for young people,so it is crucial that they continue to make real and sustained improvements in access .The social class gap among those entering higher education is unacceptably wide.Those from the top three social classes are almost three times as likely to enter higher education as those from the bottom three.

Individual universities should be able to secure increased contributions from their graduates to supplement the substantial support that they receive from the taxpayer,subject to firm limits to protect access and fairness.

The sector has embraced lifelong learning,research,knowledge transfer,social inclusion and regional economic development.There is a broad consensus within higher education that all of these elements are both welcome and necessary.However,it is unreasonable to expect all higher education institutions to sustain all of these activities simultaneously at global,and not just national,levels of excellence.No higher education system in the world is organised in this way.Rather,scarce resources are applied in such a way as to produce a focus on comparative advantage:individual institutions focus on what they do best,while the sector as a whole achieves this much wider range of objectives.

There is already a great deal of diversity within the sector.But it needs to be acknowledged and celebrated,with institutions both openly identifying and playing to their strengths. Governments of many countries accept that the state has been partly responsible for the failure to have an honest recognition of universities ' different roles. For example,institutions have in large measure been driven towards greater involvement in research by the incentives in the funding mechanisms,and by the criteria for being awarded the status of a university.

One of the results of universities acting as if they all had the same mission has been that institutions across the sector view each other as competitors;more diversity will make collaboration easier as institutions with complementary missions associate.

Having presented a radical picture of a freer future,it is the duty of government to make sure that the transition is managed carefully and sensibly so that change is not destabilising.So in some areas government will want to support the way in which institutions move towards new freedoms,and develop new patterns of provision. Government also has to retain a role because it is the only body that can balance competing interests between the different stakeholders.It will also have a responsibility to intervene when universities fail to provide adequate opportunities or when access,quality or standards are at risk.

Higher education sector is the basic unit facilaitating to meet the needs of the economy in terms of trained people,research,and technology transfer.At the same time it needs to enable all suitably qualified individuals to develop their potential both intellectually and personally,and to provide the necessary storehouse of expertise in science and technology,and the arts and humanities which defines the civilisation and culture.

To do so, the vision is of a sector which shold:

— recognise and value universities as creators of knowledge and understanding and as engines for applying that new knowledge for the benefit of all;

— recognise their role in educating their students to live life to the full,through the acquisition of skills and through fostering imagination,creativity and contribution to society;

— build strong and purposeful collaborations,including with one another and with further education,to support the best teaching,research management and knowledge transfer;

— support institutions which can compete with the best in the world in research;

— meet the developing needs of students for new modes of study and delivery of courses as well as pastoral and learning support;

— offer the opportunity of higher education to all those who have the potential to benefit;

— employ sufficient staff of the right calibre to achieve its missions,and which recruits, develops,retains and rewards them adequately;

The best universities contain a critical mass of research groups which can compete globally in a wide range of disciplines. Increased funding on its own is not enough to ensure these institutions can stay at the cutting edge.They also need the leadership,governance and management to put in place outstanding research planning,sound policies with respect to intellectual property,and a willingness to collaborate with others,and to help exploit the knowledge they generate. The

Lambert Review of links between higher education and business will ask business for its views on the present governance,management and leadership arrangements and their effectiveness in supporting good research and knowledge transfer and providing relevant skills for the economy.

Where they have these arrangements in place in addition to the critical mass of excellent research,we will allocate additional capital funding to allow them additional flexibility to achieve their institutional goals for research.

Though it is right to focus resources on the best,we must also make sure that the allocation of funding overall encourages and rewards promising departments with comparatively low research ratings,particularly for work in new research areas,so that they have the resources to develop and improve.

Research in the arts and humanities is of vital importance to the university system and its international standing. In UK research in the arts and humanities is funded by the Arts and Humanities Research Board (AHRB)(as well as through HEFCE),rather than by a research council. In September 2001,the Uk Government and devolved administrations launched a review of arts and humanities funding.The aim of the review was to enhance provision of arts and humanities research,and to ensure that there are no artificial barriers to interdisciplinary work between the arts and sciences,as well as to make sure that the arts and humanities are properly resourced and supported. This review concluded that the AHRB should take on the status of a fully fledged research council funded by the Office of Science and Technology in the same way as the other research councils.

In a knowledge-based economy both the economic competitiveness and improvements in the quality of life depend on the effectiveness of knowledge sharing between business and higher education.Good business links should also play a part in tackling the low skills levels that hold back national productivity.Much has been done through specific schemes and the Higher Education Innovation Fund to improve these links.As a result,they are already excellent in some places,but good links are neither extensive nor consistent enough.To improve,institutions should increasingly be embedded in their regional economies,and closely linked with the emerging agendas of Regional Development Agencies.The nature of the role will depend upon each institution 's mission and skills:for some it will be mainly national,for some closer to home. But in all cases,universities and colleges are key drivers for their regions,both economically and in terms of the social and cultural contribution they make to their communities.

Stronger partnerships will be encouraged between HE institutions in each region and the RDA and other agencies charged with promoting economic development.This will include RDAs being given a stronger role in steering the Higher Education Innovation Fund. There will be additional funding within the HEIF programme to set up a network of up to 20 Knowledge Exchanges to promote the critical role of less research-intensive HE institutions in transferring technologies and knowledge,and in skills development,within local communities of practice.

Knowledge and skill transfer between business and higher education is of great importance in England 's regional economies. Universities have a role in fostering the establishment and growth of new companies;in working with existing companies both on the application of the latest technology and the successful application of more tried and tested technologies;and in working with business to develop the skills of the workforce at technical and professional levels.At their best,these links should be highly interactive,with each partner well aware of what the other can offer,and of what their needs are.

The involvement of universities and colleges in regional,social and economic development is critical.Their work in knowledge and skills transfer is not their only contribution. Institutions are significant employers in local and regional economies.In addition they have a key leadership role,are often engaged in community capacity building and regeneration and make an important contribution to civil society.Higher education 's contribution to regional development very much depends on forging partnerships between institutions in each region and the RDA – as well as with other partners involved in regional skills,,business,and economic development,such as the local Learning and Skills Council.

Across the world,these partnerships are already growing.the higher education sector is actively engaged,along with other key partners,in the development of Regional Economic Strategies and has an important role to play in taking forward the new Frameworks for Regional Employment and Skills Action.It also has a key part to play in working with RDAs to identify the sort of business clusters that need to be fostered in their area.The RDAs are collaborating closely with universities on specific development and technology projects.They are also drawing on their new financial flexibilities to increase expenditure on knowledge transfer and innovation projects in which higher education institutions are in the lead or are key partners,and are helping to fund development of foundation degrees and other skills programmes.

The Governments welcome the moves that RDAs have made to build on the contribution of higher education to regional economies and is keen to support the strengthening of HE-RDA partnerships. .RDAs already have a direct input into determining new higher education provision in their regions to ensure it meets regional priorities; to involve RDAs further in the AimHigher campaign,to help address regional needs for access to higher education; to encourage RDAs to play a proactive role in developing the work of the New Technology

Higher education has a critical role to play in the community,both as a social and cultural centre and as a community leader.In some cases,universities and colleges working to serve a region together can make a dramatic impact on their community.

The relationship between knowledge transfer and the development of technical skills in the workforce,is one of interdependence:the development of new skills can also lead to a more intelligent demand for knowledge transfer and stimulate the further development of the knowledge pool.Good higher education business links should play a part in tackling the problem of low skills that holds back the national productivity.

Higher education already makes a huge contribution to the development of the higher level technical skills that are so vital.Many of the newer universities have a strong vocational focus and have led the way in developing new courses aimed at supplying students with the skills and knowledge they need for jobs in the new,expanding areas of the economy.Growth in these subjects has been substantial.Between 1995 and 1998,the number of students graduating in design studies grew overall by 32 per cent,and in computer studies by 21 per cent.Across the higher education sector,many universities are building key employability skills into courses,as well as providing short courses to help with the continuous professional development of people already in the workforce who need to keep up with the latest changes in their field.

Establishing close relationships between employers in particular industrial sectors and the relevant faculties in institutions is critical to preparing new entrants to the workforce and to continuous professional development.

Teaching and learning are central to the purpose of higher education.We are committed to understanding better where and how good teaching and learning take place and to take steps to ensure that standards are high and continually improved,and that best practice is effectively shared.All students are entitled to high quality teaching,and to the best possible information to help them make the right choices about what to study and where.And those who teach well are entitled to have their success rewarded properly.

All students are entitled to be taught well,and to be given the support they need to learn effectively.And in an era when students are being asked to contribute more to the costs of their tuition,to reflect the benefits it brings them,their expectations of teaching quality will rise. Student choice will be an increasingly important driver of teaching quality,as students choose the good-quality courses that will bring them respected and valuable qualifications and give them the higher-level skills that they will need during their working life.But student choice can only drive quality up successfully if it is underpinned by robust information – otherwise reputations will be built on perception rather than reality..And it must also be supported by clear expectations about the standards that every university must meet,so that no student has to put up with poor teaching.There must also be clear and visible rewards for the best,to spread good practice in the system,as well as sending important signals both to students and to institutions about the value of teaching in its own right.

To become intelligent customers of an increasingly diverse provision,and to meet their own increasing diverse needs,students need accessible information.

Students decide which HEIs to apply to,and employers decide which to recruit from, based on a wide range of different factors.Students take account of information from family, friends,and careers advisers,and not just about the academic aspects of different institutions and courses.Choices are bound to be complex;but the quality of the institution 's teaching should be a very important consideration.Neither students nor employers should have to base their decisions on perceptions of relative prestige which may be outdated or unreliable,but should be able to draw on up to date and robust assessments of the quality of learning and teaching.

All students have the right to good teaching,and some may not be able to exercise their choices as easily as others – perhaps because they want to study a very specialised course,,or because they would prefer to live at home.So as well as making sure that students can make well-informed choices,we must seek to guarantee good-quality teaching for everyone.This means being clearer about the teaching and learning practices and standards that students and government,as the principal funders,have a right to expect from all higher education providers.All providers should set down their expectations of teachers with reference to national professional standards;should ensure that staff are trained to teach and continue to develop professionally;should have effective quality assurance systems and robust degree standards;and should value teaching and reward good teachers.

At present,there are no nationally recognised professional standards for teachers in higher education;and many of those who teach have never received any training in how to do so.In order that teaching in higher education is treated seriously as a profession in its own right,and that teachers are given the skills they need,we expect that national professional standards will be agreed by 2004 –05,through the proposed new teaching quality academy,described below. These standards,to be designed and agreed by the sector itself,would then describe competences required for all teaching staff.Training of new staff to meet the standards should be possible through a wide range of different programmes and courses,as best suited to the institution and individual concerned.

External examiners carry out a critical role in advising institutions on the comparability of their standards,and in many respects act as guardians of the public purse and of the reputation of higher education.A key piece of information will be available through the publication of summaries of the judgements of external examiners, giving students,parents and employers access to independent views about the standards achieved on individual courses.If these reports are to be of the highest possible standard,we need to ensure that external examiners are appropriately trained and supported,by making improvements on three fronts: first,by strengthening the training given by institutions,both to enable staff to fulfil their roles as internal examiners,and to prepare them to take on the role of external examining; second,by ensuring that institutions consistently provide full briefing and induction to their newly appointed external examiners;and finally,by the sector establishing a national development programme for external examiners.

In the past,rewards in higher education – particularly promotion – have been linked much more closely to research than to teaching.Indeed,teaching has been seen by some as an extra source of income to support the main business of research,rather than recognised as a valuable and high-status career in its own right.This is a situation that cannot continue.Institutions must properly reward their best teaching staff;and all those who teach must take their task seriously.

The recent annual HEFCE survey conducted in UK provided evidence of a worrying rise in unfilled vacancies across the university workforce.Among academics,particular recruitment difficulties were reported in a range of subjects (IT/computing,business-related subjects,professions allied to medicine, science,and engineering)where higher salaries were on offer elsewhere. At the same time,as reported in the recent Roberts review,there are anecdotal reports of a decline in the quality of new applicants for academic jobs. The Government invested £50 million in 2001 – 02,£110 million in 2002 –03 and has planned for £170 million for 2003 –04 to underpin the recruitment,retention and reward plans set out in HEIs ' human resources strategies..HEFCE has distributed this money to institutions in return for human resource strategies that address issues of recruitment and retention,staff and management development,equal opportunities,rewarding good performance and tackling poor performance.This process has successfully kick-started the modernisation of human resource management in higher education,allowing institutions to play to their strengths and reward excellence.

At present,the 'University ' title is reserved for institutions that have the power to award both taught degrees,and research degrees.The right to award research degrees requires that the institution demonstrate its strength in research.This situation is at odds with the belief that institutions should play to diverse strengths,and that excellent teaching is,in itself, a core mission for a university. It is clear that good scholarship,in the sense ofremaining aware of the latest research and thinking within a subject,is essential for good teaching,but not that it is necessary to be active in cutting-edge research to be an excellent teacher.

Global economy is becoming ever more knowledge-based – we are increasingly making the living through selling high-value services,rather than physical goods.These trends demand a more highly-skilled workforce.Forecasts by the Institute for Employment Research show that between 1999 and 2010 the number of jobs in higher level occupations – the ones most likely to be filled by those who have been through higher education – will grow by over one and a half million..

That represents 80 per cent of new jobs over the decade.Almost half of these jobs will be at the associate professional and higher technician level – best served through effective work—focused programmes. The economy also needs people with modern skills at all levels.We are not choosing between more plumbers and more graduates.

There is compelling evidence that education increases productivity,and moreover that higher education is the most important phase of education for economic growth in developed countries,with increases in HE found to be positively and significantly related to per capita income growth.The review also found that education is highly likely to give rise to further indirect effects on growth, by stimulating more effective use of resources,and more physical capital investment and technology adoption.

Higher education qualifications are more than a signal to the labour market – they bring real skills benefits which employers are prepared to pay a significant premium for.The fact that studying different subjects brings different labour market benefits (which can 't be explained by the qualifications the students began the course with)argues strongly that employers are responding to real and significant skills and qualities resulting from higher education qualifications.

For the individual,the economic benefits of higher education are well-documented – quite apart from the opportunity for personal and intellectual fulfilment.Graduates and those who have 'sub-degree ' qualifications earn,,on average,around 50 per cent more than non-graduates. Graduates are half as likely to be unemployed,and as a group they have enjoyed double the number of job promotions over the last five years,compared to non-graduates. Higher education also brings social benefits – there is strong evidence that suggests that graduates are likely to be more engaged citizens.

The skills gap is most acute at a level that is served well by what has traditionally been termed 'sub-degree ' provision – two year provision that is work-focused.Jobs at the associate professional and higher technician level will experience the greatest growth in the coming years,increasing by 790,000 up to 2010.The Employer Skills Survey 2002 found that associate professional occupations were a 'hot-spot ' for skills shortage vacancies..

But work-focused higher education courses focused on this skill level have suffered from social and cultural prejudice against vocational education.Employers claim that they want graduates whose skills are better fitted for work;but the labour market premium they pay still favours traditional three-year honours degrees.Graduates with honours degrees earn 64 per cent more than those without degrees,but including two-year work-focused courses,the figure drops to 50 per cent.And students have therefore continued to apply for three-year honours courses in preference.

New foundation degrees are making a good start as a reputable and truly employer-focused higher education qualification.

In order to get over the barrier of unfamiliarity and suspicion with which new courses are often regarded,and catalyse a change in the pattern of provision in the sector,we also intend to incentivise both the supply of and the demand for foundation degrees.

Further education colleges already play an important role in delivering higher education –they currently deliver 11 per cent of higher education. Further education has strengths in providing ladders of progression for students, particularly for those pursuing vocational routes,and serves the needs of part-time students and those who want to study locally.Further education colleges make an important contribution to meeting local and regional skills needs,including through the higher education they provide.

Many further education colleges are working effectively with partner universities which formally award the foundation degrees they offer.In the best partnerships,these universities actively support the programmes and offer a real guarantee of quality to the student.However, not all further education colleges have local universities in the position to develo egree programmes with them in such a close and supportive way.

As part of making it easier to form sensible partnerships across the further education/higher education boundary,government will remove unnecessary bureaucracy where provision crosses sectors and will provide equity for both providers and learners. We believe that there are unnecessary difficulties for collaboration between higher education and further education presented by the need to respond to the two different funding council regimes in relation to planning,funding,and data collection,as well as the difficulties of juggling the requirements of the two quality assurance and inspection arrangements.Different 'mixed economy ' institutions and federal arrangements are developing where the traditional boundaries are no longer relevant or desirable.

Education must be a force for opportunity and social justice,not for the entrenchment of privilege.The opportunities that higher education brings should be available to all those who have the potential to benefit from them,regardless of their background.This is not just about preventing active discrimination;it is about working actively to make sure that potential is recognised and fostered wherever it is found.

Success in opening up higher education to all who have the potential to benefit from it depends on building aspirations and attainment throughout all stages of education.Higher education institutions need to be supported in their efforts to reach out to students from non-traditional backgrounds,and provide them with the right pastoral and teaching support;young people and their families need to be encouraged to raise their aspirations and achieve more of their potential in examinations prior to entry to higher education;and finally,there must be an effective and fair system of student support that takes into account the different circumstances of an increasingly varied student population.

3 The single most important cause of the social class division in higher education participation is differential attainment in schools and colleges.While around 43 per cent of 18 year olds from higher socio-economic backgrounds gain two or more A-levels,only 19 per cent of those from lower socio-economic backgrounds do so.Given that 9 out of 10 people with 2 or more A-levels go on to higher education by the time they are 21,this shows why the reforms to raise standards across the piece in education,beginning in early childhood and going on through schools and colleges,are so important

to the higher education agenda. It is worth noting that students from lower socio-economic groups who do achieve good A-levels are as likely to go on to university as young people from better-off backgrounds.

Standards have risen dramatically in primary schools and a substantial reform programme is now taking place in secondary education.

The Government is making an unprecedented investment in the universities and will stand by them in future spending reviews.But to be really successful,universities must be free to take responsibility for their own strategic and financial future.Strong leadership and management, freed from excessive red tape,will help them not just to respond to change,but to drive it. And more financial freedom will allow them to fund their plans,and unleash their power to drive world-class research,innovative knowledge transfer,excellent teaching,high-quality, greater and more flexible provision,and fair access.

Universities are multi-million pound organisations with a vast array of different functions and components.They must split their resources between providing the capital infrastructure for both teaching and research,compete for the best staff,and often act as both landlord and major social centre for a large body of students.They have a key role within their communities and in their contribution to community leadership.In such a complicated environment,management poses exceptional challenges and, given the return to the economy,it is only right that the Government should seek to provide help where it can.Universities need the full range of professional skills among their managers and administrators.

Although there is some excellent leadership and management in the sector,some weaker institutions have been propped up rather than turned round.This is not in the interests of the student or the sector as a whole.There is still more scope to rationalise resources to improve cost effectiveness.Institutions are increasingly entering into strategic alliances and pooling their facilities.The sector is already starting to view institutional mergers, as a path to success rather than as a response to failure.Mergers can considerably enhance an institution 's standing in the academic community and increase its capacity to generate revenue from a number of sources.

Structural change can be a formidable undertaking.We are creating a strategic development fund to support change.The fund will support structural change including strategic alliances,merger and collaboration between higher education institutions,and between higher education and further education.It will also offer incentives for institutions to develop innovative programmes of study departing from the traditional 3 year full time model.

Funding for higher education has to be made sustainable for the long term,not just the life of this spending review, and we need a system that enables universities to build up both their funding and their independence.Universities need to compete in the world market,and leading universities in other countries will be able to draw on extensive private funding.

There is a general recognition among the universities that although they look to the Government to fund teaching and research,it is unrealistic to expect the Government to match the total funding levels of the world 's best-endowed universities.It follows that giving greater financial freedom to the universities will mean increasing the financial underpinning of the sector;widening the number and type of sources of finance available to it;and reducing dependence on government.

The way forward is through endowment.This will ensure the sector is less dependent on any single source of funding,as well as enabling it to take advantage of new opportunities that they could not otherwise afford.Endowment funds can be used,for example,to make financial.investments;invest in new facilities,enabling universities to bid for research funds where the infrastructure costs are not covered;pay for specific chairs or general academic posts;undertake research,and pay researchers competitively and create scholarship funds.\

The professionalisation of fundraising activities can also be a driver for good financial management.Donors want tangible evidence of how their money has been used,and what could not be done without it.In order to gain funds the organisation has to be demonstrably excellent both in its fundraising and in its management of those given funds.

Endowment funds have the potential to provide universities with increased resources and freedoms.But inevitably it will take a long time for endowments to build up to levels which make a significant contribution to revenue.In the short term the government is putting in very significant extra funding to reverse the decline in the universities but there are,of course, competing pressures on public spending – not least provision for early years,,schools and post-16 learning.

Higher Education : Relevance Today

The relevance of higher education is considered primarily in terms of its role and place in society, its functions with regard to teaching, research and the resulting services, as well as in terms of its links with the world of work in a broad sense, relations with the state and public funding and interactions with other levels and forms of education.' The question of relevance arises even more strongly during periods of change when paradoxical situations abound and when the forces in society pull different ways. At such times, higher education must more than ever play a fundamental role by placing all its resources and its spirit of independence in the service of what is relevant to humanity and society in general.

The role of politicians is first of all to define the broad outlines of an overall development policy for the zone (province, country or region) for which they are responsible and to ensure consistency between the various development sectors and components. One of the essential functions of higher education is to give politicians, members of governments and also parliaments the relevant information stemming from their research activities, so that all parties concerned may make the proper choices in full knowledge of the facts.

When politicians and higher education meet, both must be clear about their roles: that of the politician is to make choices and to decide on guidelines on the basis of well-founded opinions; the role of higher education is to analyse, evaluate and anticipate according to criteria of truth and justice. Higher education fails in its duty when it neglects its functions of vigilance and consciousness-raising or fails to analyse the major issues confronting society.

Analyses and evaluations of changes in society and of the effects of policies mean that higher education must attribute great importance to consultation and to the critical analysis of data bases when they are available or to the establishment of such data bases when they are lacking. Here again, higher education must ensure that partnership agreements are struck with the authorities concerned by such data bases and must clarify with those authorities the ethical rules for their use.

The role of politicians is also to allocate the resources they manage in a manner consistent with the main guidelines laid down, and equitably between the various sectors. In a world where the pressures of economic liberalism are very strong, the politician must ensure that resources are properly shared between the economic and social sectors so that the economic side serves the social side and not vice versa. For its part, higher education must realize that if it undertakes its tasks properly it will be a very important vehicle for economic and social development. For it is higher education that trains the leaders of tomorrow.

From its midst are recruited most decision-makers and politicians. It is responsible for training the majority of teachers, educators and researchers. It is therefore entitled to claim the resources needed to address such important tasks, just as the politician is entitled to demand an account of the share taken up by higher education in the country's development, given the available resources.

Among the obstacles to a harmonious meeting between the state and higher education must be mentioned the often cumbersome nature of the legal and juridical structures governing higher education. The regional conferences mentioned the inertia of certain administrations, the slowness of reactions, the fussiness of certain checks and even pressures from some authorities to obtain privileges. In some regions of the world where private higher education is highly developed, a marked imbalance is found between public institutions, which are often subject to such dysfunctionality, and private institutions, which are highly flexible in their operation and insufficiently restrained by the demands of overall harmonization policy. The Havana Regional Conference called for a reform of legal and juridical structures and for consultation at regional level leading to their harmonization.

The globalization of the world economy, the increasing size of multinational companies, their international influence and the increasing difficulty of maintaining their policies, the modernization of production processes involving an increase in the educational level of an increasingly large part of the labour force and the headlong advance of technology bringing with it a need for lifelong training represent changes which are bringing higher education into increasingly frequent contact with the world of work. One of the first fruits of such contact lies in the fact that the business world can bring to higher education its entrepreneurial spirit, its concern for effectiveness and efficiency, its feeling for competition and its attention to skill; conversely, the world of higher education can contribute to business the wisdom stemming from its legendary impartiality regarding phenomena and appearances, its power to look ahead and concern for the long term, the multiplier effects of the results of its basic research and its concern for the universality of what is true and just for the development of a more harmonious world.

As their very existence is liable to be affected from day to day, businesses are accustomed to adapt to changes in the market, and they even try to nudge it in a direction favourable to them. The higher education institutions, particularly those in the public domain, have no such powerful incentives. This is particularly true as regards the task of teaching (competition between leading-edge research centres, however, is very strong). Yet it is essential that higher education should adapt to changes in the world of work, although without losing its special identity and its priorities regarding the long-term needs of society.

One of the first changes concerns curricula, which are too often directed at piling up knowledge. While there was a time not too long ago when one person could master all the knowledge existing in a particular field, this is now impossible: knowledge in chemistry doubles in less than six years; in informatics it doubles in less than five months. It is necessary for the emphasis now placed on the transmission of knowledge to switch to the process for generating it. More than ever, higher education must adopt a reactive and proactive attitude towards the labour market by analysing, forecasting and preparing for the emergence of new areas and forms of employment. Here, too, university research must acquire data bases in order to observe, analyse and anticipate trends in the world of work more effectively.

Side by side with major companies with subsidiaries in many countries, there are numerous SMFs providing a multiplicity of jobs. While more difficult to study because of their numbers, varied nature and less formal status, they are still an important field of economic activity in both the developed and the developing countries. Higher education should give them more importance and promote more constructive relations with them. Likewise, highly developed informal economies in the poorest countries should be another important field of study with the aim of better understanding their emergence, the way they operate, the way they develop in-house skills, their contribution to the country's development or under-development, the values of solidarity or, conversely, the exploitation phenomena to which they give rise.

Partnerships with firms both great and small are increasingly necessary at both basic-training and continued training levels, the latter being destined to assume even greater scope in the future. The joint organization of training courses, cost sharing for certain types of training, linked work and training, the mutual lending of both human and material resources and technological transfers represent potential fields for partnership to be developed in a spirit of respect for the specific characteristics of each partner's tasks. This means helping to train graduates who, having learnt to learn and undertake, are in a position to generate their own jobs. It means encouraging higher education to develop projects which will assist the creation of new businesses. 'Business incubator enterprises must be established with support from governments, the productive and service sectors and local communities. It means further promoting the recruitment of local graduates by international companies and contributing in this way to the reduction of unemployment among higher education graduates.

With a few rare exceptions, the initial training of teachers and many social workers is the responsibility of higher education. This is an important responsibility involving an active approach aimed at bringing higher education into touch with the other levels of the education system so as to form an 'educational chain'. This contact becomes necessary if we want the education system to form a consistent whole whose subsystems or levels are structured around a common educational project which is itself geared to the interests of a project for harmonious and sustainable development over space and time.

A permanent concern of all parties should be the necessity for high-quality basic education accessible to all and secondary education that will help prepare students to take courses at higher levels, as well as to give them immediate training for active life by qualifying them to embark on a broad spectrum of activities. Given the given impact of the role of education in development, academic research must take as one of its priorities the analysis and assessment of the various levels of the education system in close touch with the world of work without subordinating itself to it, and as part of a blueprint for society in which humanity and the collective well-being are the centre of attention. Such research must be essentially multidisciplinary because the economic and social components are closely linked; we must therefore not underestimate the importance of developing high-quality research in the social sciences on this basis.

One of the meeting-points between higher education and the other education levels is, undeniably, continuous teacher training. Knowledge is evolving at an ever-increasing pace; teachers need refresher courses. Contexts and needs change and the school cannot remain indifferent. IT is invading all areas of life; it is therefore becoming a basic tool in which education is necessary as early as primary school. Networks are multiplying in all sectors; schools must organize themselves accordingly with the assistance of higher education experts. Pedagogical research has made enormous strides in recent decades and it is for the higher education institutions to pass on the results acquired through a deliberate policy of ongoing training.

Culture is a constant quest for the true, the beautiful and the just in places of all types and in never identical epochs. It is a heritage which must not be lost and the quest for which must list it as a precious asset; it is also a heritage which must be dispersed more widely and made to yield fruit in order to press ahead with the quest for the universal through this plurality of forms. Science, education and culture are inseparable, as proclaimed in the UNESCO Charter. Just as the identity of every healthy human being is built up through a complex process of identification and differentiation and not of fusion with the Other, so the identity of a healthy human community is built up through a process both of identification with a specific culture and of differentiation, not opposition, with respect to other cultures. Just as a fulfilled person is a being who is constantly evolving, so a specific culture is not fixed but is built up by contact with other cultures.

At Jomtien in 1990, the final declaration expressed the hope that education for all would be a reality by the year 2000. However, even though school attendance rates have risen overall, they are stagnating and even falling back in certain regions of the world where structural adjustment policies have been carried out at the expense of social needs and where genocidal campaigns have led to the disappearance of up to 50% of the teaching body. Yet the need and demand for education are growing remorselessly under the twofold pressure of population growth in the developing regions and the desire to raise the overall educational level for the sake of better development and an assured place in world competition.

Population projections suggest that the world population will continue to increase from the present figure of around 5.5 billion to a population of between 11 and 14 billion by the end of the next century. Although average population growth rates are declining worldwide, the present populations continue to rise in developing regions where efforts to reduce fertility levels have met with limited success. Unless rapid population growth can be reduced, additional pressure will be put on natural and environmental resources and governance problems will increase.

Over the past two decades, higher education has undergone dramatic and quite fundamental change and many of the forces which produced these changes continue to operate. Particularly important have been quantitative expansion in student enrolments, funding constraints and privatization, reorganization of systems and diversification in structures and changes in curriculum design and delivery.

The challenges are therefore enormous, especially as the preparatory regional conferences, while calling for the most extensive democratization, urge that 'Member States should take on principal responsibility for funding for higher education... We strongly advise that the economic conditions of families be taken into consideration and that the only criteria for access or non-access should be merit.' The Latin American Conference stressed the need to 'ensure that advanced education is universal, that it offers a high quality and that it is permanently subject to revision, so as to increase the spaces for new generations'.

Access for all combined with the need to promote lifelong education calls for greater flexibility and considerable diversification in higher education training arrangements. 'Governments must expand and diversify opportunities for every citizen to benefit from higher-level skills, training, knowledge and information which are the qualifications for entry into the world of work.' This diversification must take varied forms: '...greater emphasis on a regionalization of specific disciplines. This could be a means of getting institutions to serve the specific needs of disadvantaged areas and groups. These programmes should target specific needs that will generate employment or create jobs: training programmes and structures should be flexible in order to adapt rapidly to changing needs. It would also be necessary to develop a wider variety of short duration programmes'.

Modern information and communications technology provides considerable promise to enhance teaching and learning in higher education by both on-campus and distance education students, and disabled students who tend to be denied access to technical and scholarly information resources, and to facilitate communications among researchers and teachers. Already the notion of the virtual university is being actively explored within the region. At the same time, harnessing this technology will require considerable investment in hardware, software and staff development, while deliberate efforts to ensure that the human and social interaction elements are not undervalued.

The nature itself of contemporary knowledge – in a process of constant renewal and most sudden and dramatic growth – fully agrees with the current notion of permanent education ... permanent education should also enable any person – at whatever stage of his/her life – to go back to the classrooms and find in them the opportunity to be a part of the academic life once again'. new policies and new paradigms for higher education founded on such concepts as lifelong education.

Establishments will have to turn into pertinent centres for facilitating professions to be up to date, duly retrained and reconverted. Hence they will have to offer a solid training in the basic disciplines, along with a wide diversification of programmes and studies, intermediate diplomas and links between courses and subjects. This permanent education implies that 'it is essential to define the links in the overall 'educational chain' and the relations between them so that individuals can independently manage their learning at whatever level'. This also implies 'a new approach to curriculum development, taking into account multi- and inter-disciplinarity and flexibility of choice but in a coherent system which allows for modularization, credit transfer, the validation of work experience and the organization of the academic year in semesters'.Programmes must be organized so as to stimulate the entrepreneurial abilities of students based on flexible, innovating and interdisciplinary approaches.

Getting together with the student is more than a problem of access; it is also one of genuinely meeting the student as an evolving person and being. Beyond the formal curricula, the environment in which the student moves is an educational or anti-educational factor. A dirty environment is no sort of training in environmental concern or a feeling for the beautiful. An environment where a frantic spirit of competition prevails does not educate in solidarity. An environment where teachers do not respect their commitments (unjustified absences, delays, etc) does not educate in responsibility. Higher educational institutions must be designed and managed as educational spaces and not only as places of training.

A changing society demands people to have a comprehensive, general and professional education. The latter must encourage the development of a person as a whole and should favour his/her personal growth, autonomy, socialization and the skills to turn the assets that perfect it into elements having real value. This integral training and the acquisition of an entrepreneurial spirit begin with the active participation of the students not only in education activities but also in the management and life of higher education institutions: student involvement in decision-making bodies should be given a considerable boost.

Higher education institutions must be made more aware of students' concerns by taking their needs into account and adopting measures enabling them to play an active part in decision-making processes in the institutions. Teachers are primary resources on which depend to a great extent the relevance and quality of higher education within its three basic tasks: teaching, research and services.

Meeting the needs of teachers so that they can perform their tasks is therefore fundamental in accordance with the Recommendation concerning the Status of Higher education Teaching Personnel approved by the General Conference of UNESCO in November 1997. This means, first of all, managing careers on the basis of merit, i.e. of profiles of required skills. 'Governments, Parliaments and institutions of higher education should pay particular attention to the draft Recommendation concerning the Status of Higher education Teaching Personnel'. This means enabling them to maintain and update their knowledge through various initiatives, such as sabbatical years, study tours, time spent at centres of excellence, attendance at scientific meetings, networking, access to the IT. It also means allowing them to acquire the new skills required by developments in higher education.

The shift from teaching to learning implies self-managed learning, a coaching role for the teacher a new definition of scholarship balancing discovery and transmission, as well as the integration and application of knowledge. A crucial lever for change is a creative and well-defined personnel policy which opens up teaching as a career, supported by appropriate staff development programmes. Particular attention should be paid to the promotion of opportunities for women, including in top positions in higher education.

Personnel management necessarily involves the introduction of a culture of assessment but this must be done in a spirit of willingness to meet the other side halfway and take the general background into account, and thus in a spirit of instructive dialogue. Self-assessment must accompany external assessment, there must be attention to facts and results and not judgement about individuals, there must be discussion with the persons concerned of the meaning to be attached to the results, negotiation of the decisions to be taken and contracts agreed, without forgetting follow-up.

The potential impact of higher education on a country's development stands in no further need of proof. Imbalances between the various regions of the world are increasing. Within the developing countries in particular, imbalances of all sorts (between urban and rural areas, between the sexes, between minorities and majorities, etc.) are persisting or becoming more acute.

Higher education institutions do not possess the financial and human resources to respond in isolation and with a quality level sufficient to meet all needs and demands. A joint internationalization and contextualization policy is therefore necessary at both the education and research levels. Internationalization implies increased networking, which means that institutions must carry out a whole series of operations and communicate the results among themselves by making use of advances in information and communication technology:

— identification of strong and weak sectors in the field of both education and research (both tasks are closely linked);

— the grading of local and national needs according to importance;

— identification of priority needs which can be met with the existence of an adequate critical mass of resources in quantitative and qualitative terms and, conversely, those that cannot be met;

— identification of potential complementarities inside and outside the country; development of a policy which, instead of scattering resources, focuses them on the creation of local, national or international centres of excellence situated in one and the same place or operating on an exchange basis or even at a distance, as the case may be;

— a policy of linking these centres of excellence around a coherent project conceived as a development process lasting several years.

Such internationalization, however, must go hand in hand with contextualization, i.e. the taking into account of the presence of important specific goals, of standards specific to certain contexts, and of differentiated conditions for accomplishing the tasks of education and research. Excessive emphasis on applied research in response to immediate needs is liable to dry up the principal source for the development of knowledge and its transfer to applied research and research and development. An over-emphasis on basic research means taking the risk of isolating oneself from the needs of the world of work and society or assigning this task exclusively to bodies whose concern for short-term profitability does not help sustainable development; it also means ignoring the increasingly obvious fact that the distinction between the two types of research is becoming ever more tenuous and that numerous questions of fundamental research arise from problems originally posed by applied research.

Higher education must pay greater heed to mixing the various disciplines. Genuinely interdisciplinary research spawns the new disciplines of tomorrow and is more likely to be relevant to industrial opportunities and the resolution of industrial or societal problems. One challenge is how to stimulate interdisciplinary research proactively when institutions are normally organized on discipline-based departments and when much external evaluation reinforces this, by itself reviewing disciplines and implicitly discouraging interdisciplinary connections.

The rigid disciplinary boundaries between the hard sciences and the social sciences and the humanities that limited the comprehension of the fundamental processes of nature and society are already breaking down in some fields. There must be a stimulus to the creation of interdisciplinary programmes, and resources must be ensured for collaborative research among different disciplines and involving groups around thematic projects. Moreover, as pointed out by experts from the Council of Europe meeting in July 1998. By becoming the main source of wealth for individuals and nations, science is giving higher education an increasing role in lifelong education, while simultaneously its cumulatively segregative character requires higher education to provide a counterweight to its economist tendency.

Sustainable human development cannot be brought into being without the existence of a culture of peace in places and at times at which wars, massacres, disturbances and disputes are sapping the economy, generating insecurity and strengthening imbalances. Conversely, a culture of peace cannot develop in contexts where development levels are tending to stagnate or even fall back, and where private short-term interests take precedence over the quest for sustainable human development for all. 'Institutions of higher education should adopt a proactive policy in this connection and invest all their energy into fighting poverty, environmental degradation, discrimination of all kinds, and the ravages of conflicts. Higher education establishments have a key role to play by contributing to equitable and sustainable development and to the culture of peace actively promoting intellectual and moral solidarity.

Universality of Higher Education

The foundations of a universal vision of higher education can be grouped together around ten closely interdependent, axiological principles forming an inseparable axiological whole, which following the theoreticians of gestalt theory could be described as a 'good axiological form'. It is the universality of higher education, together with the fact that it takes place in a particular space and time, that constitutes the basis of these ten principles in accordance with the saying 'Think globally and act locally'.

i) *The universality of higher education implies universal access for all those who have the ability and motivation (access and merit) and suitable preparation at every stage in life":* This first axiological principle, which concerns equity, is in full agreement with Article 26 of the Declaration on Human Rights: 'Everyone has the right to education (...): higher education shall be equally accessible to all on the basis of merit'. In addition, the Convention against Discrimination in Education stipulates in Article 4, paragraph a): 'make higher education equally accessible to all, on the basis of individual capacity'. Furthermore, the International Covenant on Economic, Social and Cultural Rights states in Article 13, paragraph 2 c): 'Higher education shall be made equally accessible to all, on the basis of capacity, by every appropriate means and in particular by the progressive introduction of free education'. The principle of merit as understood here concerns not only students but also the academic staff of higher education institutions without distinction as to sex, religion, geographical, social or ethnic origin, political allegiance, lack of money or any other factor of discrimination. These principles confirm that access to higher education is one of the basic issues - if not the most important issue - in the process of reforming this level of education, since on it depend the policies of each country or government in this field. The reality is that inequalities regarding access persist in many countries and region.

ii) *The universality of higher education implies the use of varied forms of intervention in order to meet the educational needs of all at all stages of life*: Education for all assumes that education does not stop with schooling but extends to every phase of life in order to give a fresh chance to those who have not benefited from it, to permit the process of updating necessitated by changed situations or simply to continue one's personal development. Higher education must be viewed as a system of continuing education and training. Education for all throughout life also means that higher education must take account of the characteristics of individuals and their circumstances. It must therefore provide suitable education and training facilities: part-time training, linked work and training, distance learning, capitalizable modules, virtual universities, decentralization of training groups. Higher education exists to serve individuals and not vice versa. It must therefore take risks, try out new arrangements, fertilize these new arrangements by exchanges of experience and make full use of the potential of new technology and distance learning.

iii) *The universality of higher education implies that the latter's function is not only to train but also to educate*: It is not enough to train students or adults; higher education must go much further in educational task, i.e. it must contribute to the fulfilment of human beings in all their aspects and improve general well-being on this planet. As pointed out by the expert meeting in Toronto in April 1998, it is necessary to 'reaffirm the central task of higher education of training and educating in a long-term perspective, not only with a view to short-term adjustment to the labour market but also for personal development and with an eye to a contribution by individuals to social and economic development through citizenship education and lifelong training'. A course is never neutral; it is therefore important to use it as a vehicle for humanist values. Training courses as a whole must be viewed as preparation for better living together; higher education institutions must therefore teach their students to be entreprising, to create opportunities and not to expect a job as a right.

iv) *The universality of higher education implies that its functions include vigilance and consciousness-raising:* As a fount of training, education, expertise and research, higher education must be careful to make its intellectual resources and independence of thought available for the purposes of vigilance and consciousness-raising. These two functions consist in identifying situations, in their various economic, social, political, scientific and technological components, in which the True and the Just are flouted. They consist in anticipating the consequences of such situations. They consist, finally, in studying tendencies which affect the future of society and the scenarios that are most likely to build better and sustainable development, bearing in mind the principle that the future is constructed less according to what is technically feasible than according to what is possible and desirable socially.

v) *The universality of higher education implies that it should therefore have a guiding ethical role at a time when there is a crisis of values*: In all its activities, higher education seeks the true and must ceaselessly track down what is false, flush out fallacious arguments, and furnish proof of its statements. But it must also ceaselessly place all its activities at the service of what is just, i.e. what is in keeping with universal basic rights, in this case human rights, the rights of the child and rights concerning respect for nature and rights to a quality environment. Faced with the perverse effects of poorly understood globalization and the dangers of unbridled – that is, uncivilized – capitalism, faced, too, with the rise of selfish interests and an all-pervading relativism, higher education must proclaim loudly and clearly a scale of universal values in which the universal 'We' takes precedence over 'I', in which science and technology are employed for the benefit of all humanity and not in the selfish interests of various powerful parties, and in which solidarity comes before competition. This role begins in the higher education institutions themselves, in their method of organization and in the climate which they create in their midst.

vi) *The universality of higher education implies that throughout all its activities it must develop a culture of peace:* A culture of peace starts by respecting and making allowance for other people with all their differences, rights and duties. It implies participation, involvement, a sense of responsibility and respect for commitments. This culture of peace therefore begins within the institution itself. But working for a universal culture of peace also means that higher education must develop research on this theme (e.g. study the factors which trigger off murderous conflicts, wars, violence, disturbances, hatred, etc.) and devote an important place to it in its curriculum.

vii) *The universality of higher education implies that it must build up links of universal solidarity with other higher education institutions and other institutions of society:* In addition to the strategic alliances necessitated by international competition and by a concern for effectiveness and efficiency, higher education must develop alliances based on solidarity. These must be true examples of solidarity and not relations of dominance of weak institutions by more powerful ones. Each partner has its own riches, which are not solely material, and shares them with an eye to complementarity and to a mutual quest for equity and quality. The UNITWIN/UNESCO Chairs programme networks and the programmes of other organizations inspired by the same ideals must continue work in this spirit. It is important, too, that the universities of the North, which attract researchers from the developing countries and thereby contribute to the brain drain, should help such researchers return to the higher education institutions of those countries in a true spirit of solidarity.

vii) *The universality of higher education implies that it must develop a management method based on the dual principle of responsible autonomy and transparent accountability:* In order to discharge the different tasks already mentioned and make itself available to all, higher education must be in a position to resist pressures which might cause it to swerve from its path. This does not mean that it should take refuge in an ivory tower; on the contrary, it must ensure that it has a clear understanding with the political authorities, who are responsible for proposing development projects, concerning the part that it will be playing in them, and that it is autonomous and responsible for the internal management of such projects; at the same time, it must arrange for clear accountability at the various internal and external levels regarding the results of its activities. Responsible autonomy and accountability are two inseparable aspects of clearly understood academic freedom.

ix) *The universality of higher education implies that it should be at pains to set clear standards of quality and relevance that go beyond standards specific to particular contexts*: A quest for quality and relevance have always been features of higher education. Essentially international while forming part of a particular context, it creates links with other institutions. This implies efforts to implement curricula and qualifications that are comparable - which does not mean that they should be uniform.

x) *The universality of higher education implies that its ultimate axiological principle, subsuming all others, should be to work for the unity of women and men in mutually supportive differentiation and complementarity*

Bibliography

Altbach, P. and Teichler, U, "Internationalization and exchanges in a globalized university", *Journal of Studies in International Education*, 5, (1) 5-25, 2001.

Back, Ken, Dorothy Davis et al, *Internationalisation and Higher Education: Goals and Strategies,* Australian Government Publishing Service, Canberra, 1992.

Barnett, R., *Improving Higher Education: Total quality care,* SRHE/ Open University Press, Buckingham, 1992.

Cosh, J, Peer observation in higher education: a reflective approach, *Innovations in Education and Training International*, 35, 171-176, 1998

Currie, J., & Newson, J. (eds.), *Universities and globalization: Critical perspectives.* Thousand Oaks: Sage Publications.

Eraut, M, *Developing Professional Knowledge and Competence,* Falmer, London, 1994.

Frazer, M., *"Quality assurance and higher education"*. In A. Craft (ed), Quality assurance in higher education: proceedings of an instructional conference. London: Falmer, 1992.

Gopinathan, S., "Globalization, the state, and education policy in Singapore", *Asia Pacific Journal of Education*, 16, (1), 74-87, 1996.

Government of India, Ministry of Education, *Report of the University Education Commission* (Radhakrishnan Commission). Delhi, Manager of Publications, 1951.

Green D., *What is Quality in Higher Education ?.* S.R.H.E and Open University Press, Buckingham, 1994.

Johnes, J., and Taylor, J., *Performance Indicators in Higher Education,* SRHE and Open University-Press, Buckingham, 1990

Moonis Raza, ed. *Higher education in India; retrospect and prospect.* New Delhi, Association of Indian Universities, 1991.

Scott, P., "Globalization and higher education: Challenges for 21st century", *Journal of International Education,* 4, (1), 3-10., 2000.

United Nations Development Program (UNDP), Human development report. New York: UNDP, 1999.

World Bank, Higher Education in developing countries: Peril and promise. World Bank: Washington D.C., 2000.

World Bank, Higher education. The lessons of experience. World Bank: Washington, D.C, 1994.

Ishengoma, J.M. , "The Myths and Realities of Higher Education Globalization: A View From the Southern Hemisphere", *FOCUS JOURNAL,* Open Forum, 2003.

Index